COMPUTER IMAGING FOR
DESIGN & MERCHANDISING

NICK CASSWAY

Kendall Hunt
publishing company

Kendall Hunt
publishing company

www.kendallhunt.com
Send all inquiries to:
4050 Westmark Drive
Dubuque, IA 52004-1840

This book is dedicated to Jack Cassway
who makes me see the world differently everyday.

CONTENTS

SECTION 3 INDESIGN 85

INTRODUCTION

My teaching philosophy for computer graphics is two-fold. First, is the introduction of these essential tools and what makes them unique in relationship to traditional drawing and painting tools. The second, and equally important, is building confidence with these tools. I believe it is important to recognize that not everyone feels "at home" in front of a computer screen. Even though we all spend many hours a day using computers, some of us feel like computers hate us or that something will inevitably go wrong. Of course, others know these tools well and just need to apply their skills with some practical application. The majority of us fall in the middle—comfortable enough learning something new but not deeply familiar with the tools. Assisting all levels of students in feeling confident with computer graphics tools, whether it's overcoming their initial fear or as a natural outlet for their self-expression, is immensely important. As an educator, I sometimes forget that I am very accustomed to using these tools and that the adaptive thinking necessary to using them has become innate.

Key to the success of building confidence is providing students opportunities to explore and experiment with the tools on their own time and in their own way. Many of us learned these tools on our own and encountered frustration as well as success along our learning path. I think it's important to provide a context for students to explore these tools and to encourage those who feel apprehensive about making potential mistakes. For this to occur, it is important that all students spend a good chunk of time outside of class (preferably three hours) trying out new skills or practicing skills that have been introduced during the work session. My hope is that through a rigorous curriculum that includes opportunities to make work without fear of abject failure, as well as the ability to experiment in their own way, students will become familiar with core computer graphics tools and attain a confidence in interacting with them.

SECTION 1

Adobe Illustrator

CHAPTER 1

Learning Our Way Around, and Getting Comfortable

Adobe Illustrator is a program designed to create original artwork on a computer and allows you to draw shapes and then infinitely refine them. Adobe Illustrator is a vector drawing program; this means that lines and shapes are defined by points in space.

The Illustrator window consists of 3 main areas—the Menu (at the top of the screen), the Toolbar (typically on the left hand side) and the Panels (typically on the right or accessible from the WINDOW menu. [fig. 1.1, 1.2, 1.3]

To create a New File go to the FILE menu > NEW. [fig 1.4] or cmd/ctrl + n. From there, Illustrator will prompt you with a dialogue box to define how your new file will appear. NAME—you can name the file or leave it as *untitled* (Illustrator will prompt you for a name when you save the file); **Profile**—select what the file will be ultimately used for— **Print, Web, Devices, Film & Video, or Custom. Size**—depending on the profile, a list of predefined sizes will appear. The **Width** and **Height** are initially defined in

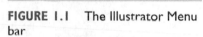

FIGURE 1.1   The Illustrator Menu bar

FIGURE 1.2   The Illustrator toolbar

FIGURE 1.3   The Illustrator Default panel bar

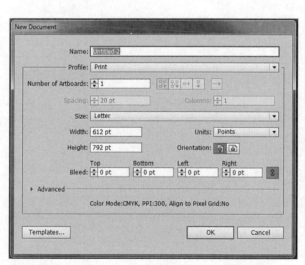

FIGURE 1.4   The New Document window

points but can be changed to any other measurement in the **Units** area. A note: points are a typographic unit of measurement but can be easily translated into inches. 1″ = 72 points. An 8 1/2″ × 11″ sheet translates into 612 pt × 792 pt; Illustrator will even do the conversion for you! Select OK when you're ready to go.

There are many, many tools in Illustrator that will be covered in later sections. It is important to recognize that there are usually at least two ways to perform functions in the program. For example: to zoom in, use the **Zoom** tool on the Toolbar [**fig 1.5**] and then click on the screen to zoom in. Additionally, you can go to the VIEW menu and click on ZOOM IN or use cmd/ctrl and the + key on the keyboard to perform the same function. A scale percentage can also be typed within the bottom left-hand side of the screen.

FIGURE 1.5   The Zoom tool

To zoom out

1.   hold the option/alt key on the keyboard along with the **Zoom** tool,
2.   go to the VIEW menu > ZOOM OUT;
3.   use the keyboard shortcut cmd/ctrl and the—key; or
4   type in a percentage.

To get back to a full view of your work area, go to the VIEW menu > FIT IN WINDOW or cmd/ctrl + 0.

CHAPTER 2

Illustrator Core Concepts

All entities in Illustrator have two basic properties, a stroke (or outline) and a fill **[fig 2.1]**. The stroke can be changed into any color, gradient, or pattern as well as no color (**none**) and can have the width of the line changed to any thickness. The fill property can also have any color, gradient, or pattern as well as **none** attributed to it. The default setting for all shapes is a white fill and a black stroke with a weight of 1 pt. To get back to default colors, type **D** on the keyboard. To switch whether the stroke or fill is the prominent attribute, type **X**.

FIGURE 2.1   The Default Illustrator colors (white fill, black stroke)

To draw a line, choose the **Pen** tool **[fig 2.2]**, or type P on the keyboard, click one point on the screen, and then click another point. At this stage the line is considered an open path; by creating more points on the screen and then returning to the first, the path will be closed. **[figs 2.3]** All shapes in Illustrator will always have the fill property whether it is open or closed, to turn off the fill property, choose none **[fig 2.4]** as the fill or type / on the keyboard.

FIGURE 2.2   The Pen tool

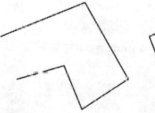

To select your objects in order to modify or transform them use the **Selection** tool also known as the **Black Arrow [fig 2.5]** (or type V on the keyboard). When an object is selected with the black arrow all of the points drawn with the pen tool will be a solid color—this means the ENTIRE object is selected. To modify individual points on an object, use the **Direct Selection** tool, also known as the white arrow **[fig 2.6]** (or type A on the keyboard). This tool will allow you to select individual points to modify; when you select an individual point, just that point will be solid, the other points will be white with an outline.

A **Solid Point** is SELECTED, an **Outlined Point** is NOT SELECTED. **[fig 2.7]**

FIGURE 2.3   An Open Path (left) and a Closed Path (right)

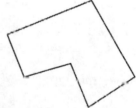

 FIGURE 2.4 "None" Fill

 FIGURE 2.5 The Selection tool, or Black Arrow

 FIGURE 2.6 The Direct Selection tool, or White Arrow

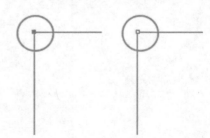

FIGURE 2.7   Selected Anchor Point (left) and Deselected Anchor Point (right)

All modifications to existing shapes follow the above rules—select the object first and then choose the modification. Any new objects drawn will have the properties (fill and stroke color, stroke thickness) of the last object drawn or modified.

Change the color of the fill by selecting the object, choose the **Fill color icon,** and then select a color, gradient, or pattern from the swatches panel. Likewise, change the stroke color by selecting the object, choose the **Stroke color icon,** and then pick a color, gradient, or pattern from the swatches panel.

To change the thickness (or weight) of the line, select the object, and then enter a new weight in the stroke panel. With all panels, there is a context menu on the upper right corner **[fig 2.8]**; click the Menu icon to **Show Options**. The stroke panel changes the width of a line as well as how end caps and corners appear. End caps can be defined as **Butt, Rounded,** or **Projected** caps. Corners can be **Mitered, Rounded** or **Beveled**. The stroke of a closed shape can be aligned to the center of the line, the outside, or the inside. By selecting Dashed Line—a customized dashed line can be created with separate widths for dashes and gaps. **[fig 2.9]**

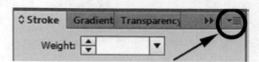

FIGURE 2.8 Context Menu for panels

To select multiple objects in your drawing, either make a selection rectangle with the **black arrow** that touches all of the objects, or select an object and then hold the SHIFT key down to add to the selection. SHIFT can also be used to remove something from a selection. This works with the **white arrow** as well to select multiple points.

To deselect objects:

1. go to the SELECT menu > DESELECT;
2. click on an empty area of your drawing; or
3. use the keyboard shortcut cmd/ctl + SHIFT + A

To delete objects, select them using the **black arrow** and use the DELETE key on your keyboard. To undo any action, go to the EDIT menu > UNDO or use cmd/ctl + Z

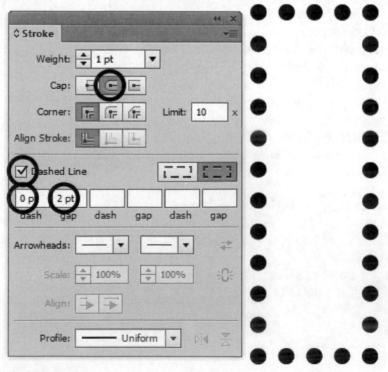

FIGURE 2.9 To make a dotted line: change the caps to ROUNDED, select DASHED LINE, change the dash to 0, and the gap to at least TWICE the line weight.

CHAPTER 3

Drawing Basic Shapes

Commands to cut, copy, and paste are located in the EDIT menu. These are similar to commands in other programs (Word, Excel, etc.) and share the same keyboard shortcuts. Cmd/ctrl + C for Copy, cmd/ctrl + X for cut, and cmd/ctrl + V for paste. In addition, Illustrator provides the ability to paste something exactly in the same location that it was copied from by using PASTE IN PLACE or cmd/ctrl + SHIFT + V.

Copying or cutting can be performed on an entire object by selecting with the **black arrow** or on points and line segments by selecting with the **white arrow.**

Illustrator provides shape tools to act as basic building blocks for drawing. These include a Rectangle, Rounded Rectangle, Ellipse, Polygon, and Star tools. **[FIG. 3.1]** All of these tools can be created in numerous ways.

FIGURE 3.1 Illustrator Shape tools

To draw a rectangle, either 1.) click and drag a rectangle on the screen; 2.) click and drag while holding the SHIFT key to make a rectangle with equal sides (a square); 3.) click and drag while holding the opt/alt key to draw the rectangle from the center; or 4.) click directly on the screen to bring up a dialog box and type in the height and width. These options are the same for all of the shape tools. **[FIG. 3.2]**

Options for the **Rounded Rectangle** include the corner radius; for the **Polygon** include a number of sides starting at three; and for the **Star** include an inner and outer radius and number of points.

NOTE: The SHIFT key performs one of two functions depending on how it is used, either to add or subtract from selections or to constrain proportions while drawing or transforming.

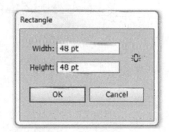

FIGURE 3.2 Rectangular shape dialog box

Use the VIEW menu > SHOW GRID to show the drawing grid. The default is a 1-inch x 1-inch grid with eight subdivisions. Use the VIEW menu > SNAP TO GRID to keep all line segments and points aligned to grid intersections.

Every object created in Illustrator has a stacking order. The first object drawn will be at the bottom of the stack and the most current object drawn will be at the top. Use the OBJECT menu > ARRANGE sub menu to control the order of the objects drawn. Choices include **Bring To Front, Bring Forward, Send Backward,** and **Send To Back. [FIG. 3.3]**

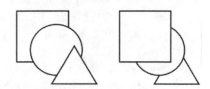

FIGURE 3.3 Original Stacking Order (left), Square Moved to Front, Triangle Moved to Back (right)

Many tools on the toolbar have further options associated with them. The **Pen** tool has options to **Add Points** or **Subtract Points** from an object. [FIG. 3.4] These options will also appear when an object is selected and the Pen tool is the current tool. If the cursor is near a line segment, the **Add Anchor Point** icon will appear. If the cursor is near an anchor point, the **Subtract Anchor Point** icon will appear.

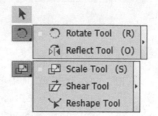

FIGURE 3.4 Pen tool options—Pen Tool, Add Anchor Point, Delete Anchor Point, Convert Anchor Point

There are five transformations that can be performed on objects in Illustrator: **Move, Scale, Rotate, Shear,** and **Reflect.** [FIG. 3.5] All of these transformations require that the object is selected before selecting the transformation. There are two major ways to perform these transformations. The first is to directly perform the operation on screen by selecting the object and then **dragging the cursor** (with mouse button depressed) to see the transformation. The second method is to select the object and then **double click** the transformation icon; this will bring up a dialogue box to type in the parameters of the transformation.

Universal options for all transformations include the ability to **preview** the transformation and **copy** the object as well as cancel and OK. The MOVE tool (the black arrow) includes options to adjust the horizontal and vertical movements; an angle and distance from the original object can also be entered. The SCALE tool includes options to **uniformly** scale the object (by percent), or **non-uniformly** scale the object in the horizontal and vertical directions. The **Rotate** tool includes options for the rotation angle. The **Shear** tool includes options for the angle of shearing and the axis for shearing (either horizontal, vertical, or an arbitrary angle) a negative number may be used as well. The **Reflect** tool includes a mirror axis—either horizontal, vertical, or an arbitrary angle.

FIGURE 3.5
Transformations—Move, Rotate, Reflect, Scale, Shear

All transformations originate by default at the center of the selected object(s). The **reference point** (a light blue target icon) is used to indicate the center of the transformation but may be moved to any location on the screen. For directly transforming on screen, drag the reference point to a new position, release the mouse button and begin the transformation. For a dialogue box transformation, hold the opt/alt key, drag the center point, release the button and option/alt key, and the dialogue box will pop up. [FIG. 3.6]

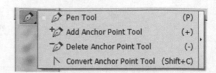

FIGURE 3.6 Holding the Alt/option key while moving the reference point with Transformations will produce a dialog box.

Transformations can be performed on the full object itself by selecting with the black arrow or can be performed on individual points or line segments by selecting those items with the white arrow.

*Note: Within transformations some movements are indicated in a counter-intuitive fashion. For instance, to move an object up using the **Move** transformation dialogue box, a negative number must be used. A positive number, however, for horizontal movements will move the object to the right. Within the **Rotate** transformation, a positive number will rotate the object counter-clockwise (to the left).*

Using the OBJECT menu > GROUP command, multiple objects can be combined so that they can be transformed as one. With the white arrow, individual components of grouped objects can be edited.

The pathfinder panel provides the ability to create complex shapes from various combinations of two or more shapes. The pathfinder panel (WINDOW menu > PATHFINDER) is broken up into two sections. On the top of the panel are shape modes that include: **Unite, Minus Front, Intersect,** and

Exclude. The pathfinders on the bottom row include: **Divide, Merge, Trim, Crop, Outline,** and **Minus Back. [FIG. 3.7]**

Unite will take two or more objects and create a new object from them; the two objects do not have to be on top of one another. **Minus Front** will subtract a shape placed on top of another shape. **Intersect** will create a shape resulting from the overlap between two shapes. **Exclude** will create shapes that are the opposite of intersect; that is, the overlapped shape will disappear while the rest of the shapes will combine. **[FIG. 3.8]**

Divide is a pathfinder that will take overlapping objects and create shapes based on where they overlap. After using the Divide pathfinder all of the objects will be grouped together; use the OBJECT menu > UNGROUP to make them into individual shapes. This will happen for all pathfinders. **Trim** will use the most forward shape as a cookie cutter, removing everything outside of its outline and dividing the shapes inside. **Merge** will combine shapes with the same fill and stroke within a selection. **Crop** will use the outline of the top shape to crop out pieces from the shapes behind it. The top most cropping shape will be retained but will have no fill or outline color. **Outline** will take the two or more intersecting shapes and create unclosed paths from them. The resulting shapes will only be linework with no stroke weight. **Minus Back** will subtract a shape from behind a shape in front. **[FIG. 3.9]**

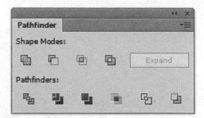

FIGURE 3.7   The Pathfinder panel

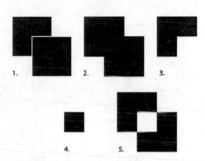

FIGURE 3.8   Shape Modes—1. Original Shapes 2. Unite 3. Minus Front 4. Intersect 5. Exclude

Use the **Align panel** to align or distribute objects. Objects can be aligned to their collective left, right, upper, or lower edge as well as their horizontal or vertical centers by using the **Align Objects** options. The align panel is found under the WINDOW menu > OBJECT & LAYOUT > ALIGN. A randomly distributed selection of objects can be evenly distributed along their left, right, upper, or lower edge as well as their horizontal or vertical centers by using the **Distribute Objects** options. Select **Use Spacing** to impose a specific amount of space between each object. **[FIG. 3.10]**

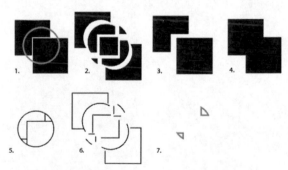

FIGURE 3.9   Pathfinders—1. Original Shapes 2. Divide 3. Trim 4. Merge 5. Crop 6. Outline 7. Minus Back

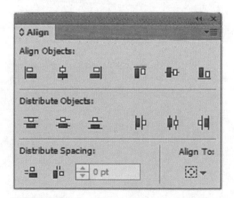

FIGURE 3.10   Align panel

CHAPTER 4

Curves and Drawing

A curve point is a point in space that creates a curved line coming into and out of the point. To create a curve, click and drag the Pen tool with the mouse button held down. The dragging action creates a pair of handles that define the shape of the curve. Dragging out a long way makes the curve steeper; a short distance makes a flatter curve. **[FIG. 4.1]**

(Note: the end of the curve handle IS NOT the end of the line, the end of the line is the last point created.)

Highlighting the curve point with the direct selection tool (white arrow) will show the two handles of the curve; these may be modified. Dragging the control point away or towards the curve point will produce the same effects as it did upon creation. Rotating the control point will change the direction of the curve. (Note: rotating one control point produces the opposite result in the other control point.) **[FIG. 4.2]** By selecting the line between two points, the shape of the line can be edited. The line shape will change but the points will remain where they are.

FIGURE 4.1 Curve handles pulled farther away from the anchor point create steeper curves; curve handles that are shorter create flatter curves.

There are two other curves—one that changes directions (handles are broken) and a hybrid point that includes a curve and a corner. To create a broken curve point, click and drag the curve point and then hold down the opt/alt key to break the relationship between the two handles; this will define a curve coming into the point and curve exiting the point, but it will not be a continuous curve. **[FIG. 4.3]** The hybrid point involves drawing a curve point and then clicking on the point with the Pen tool immediately after to define the exiting line as a straight path. **[FIG. 4.4]** Both of these types of points may be created after the fact by using the white arrow. To make a broken curve, use the white arrow and the opt/alt key on an existing handle. To make a hybrid point, simply drag the handle back to the originating point. A corner point can be changed into curve point by using the Convert Anchor Point tool (associated with the Pen tool). Use this tool by clicking on an existing point and dragging away from the point. You may use this as well to convert a curve point to a corner.

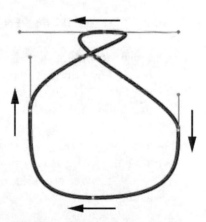

FIGURE 4.2 All shapes are drawn in either a clockwise or counter-clockwise manner. Reversing the orientation of the curve handles creates a loop.

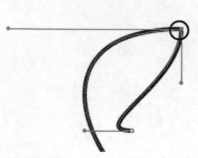

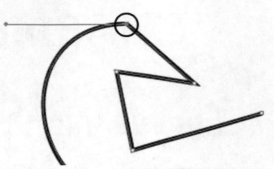

FIGURE 4.3 A "broken" curve

FIGURE 4.4 A "hybrid" point, a curve comes into the anchor point and exits as a corner point.

Points can also be added exactly halfway between existing points on a path by using OBJECT menu > PATH > ADD ANCHOR POINTS.

Break a path or shape by using the **Scissors** tool **[FIG. 4.5]** located on the toolbar. Click on an existing anchor point or anywhere along a line segment to break the shape into two.

FIGURE 4.5 The Scissors tool

Two or more open paths may be fused together as one by using the JOIN tool (OBJECT menu > PATH > JOIN). There are two ways to use this tool: 1.) select two endpoints from separate paths with the white arrow and use the **Join** command; 2.) Select two or more line segments with the black arrow and use the Join command. In either of these instances, if the endpoints are touching they will be considered as one; if they are separate then a line segment will be drawn between them.

BEST PRACTICES WITH THE PEN TOOL

Use as few points as possible when tracing and use curves where appropriate. Using the smallest number of points possible provides greater flexibility when editing the linework later. Too many points will introduce unnecessary bumps into the linework. Using curves also provides greater flexibility in the editing. Adjusting the anchor point handles is far and away much easier than adjusting many, many points.

Whenever possible, place anchor points at 90-degree angles from one another when creating curves. As a general rule place points at the extreme top, bottom, and sides of a shape and drag the handles either vertically or horizontally. The preferred method of creating points is by using CLICK + SHIFT + DRAG. This will lock the handles into 90- or 0-degree angles. **[FIG. 4.6]**

Some shapes will be

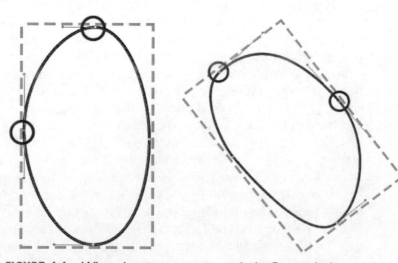

FIGURE 4.6 When drawing or tracing with the Pen tool, place anchor points on the extremes of the shape and lock them 0 and 90° angles (left). If 0 and 90° is not possible, reorient an imaginary rectangle around the shape and keep anchors at right angles (right).

impossible to use perfectly the horizontal and vertical method. In this case, rotate the imaginary box to align with the curve and drag the handles out to align with the sides. In this case, use CLICK + DRAG (no SHIFT) and attempt to keep anchor handles at right angles (where applicable). Return to 0 and 90 when appropriate.

The Pen tool and the Direct Selection tool (white arrow) work in conjunction with each other. Draw your points where you think they should go and then come back later and adjust their location and the shape of the curve with the white arrow. Understanding that corrections can be made to established linework is the key to mastering the Pen tool in Illustrator!

TRACING

To bring a sketch or photo into Illustrator in order to trace over it, use the FILE menu > PLACE. To facilitate tracing, make the sketch or photo a **Template** by going to the **layers panel** and from the CONTEXT menu choose **Template.** A new layer will be required to do the tracing; use the **Make New Layer** icon to create a new layer. **[FIG. 4.7]** The graphic can also be defined as a template by selecting the Template option on the **Place** window.

Change the **fill color** to **none** and provide a color for the stroke. A fill of none will not block out the original drawing.

Use the OBJECT menu > HIDE to temporarily make selected object invisible; use the OBJECT menu > LOCK to temporarily make the object un-selectable. Both tools have the choices of hiding or locking the current selected object or objects, hiding or locking everything above the selected object(s), or (if you are working with layers) hiding or locking everything on layers other than your current object(s). To make visible hidden objects, go to the OBJECT menu > SHOW ALL. To unlock locked objects, go to the OBJECT menu > UNLOCK ALL.

Use the OBJECT menu > PATH > CLEANUP to delete invisible objects from the drawing. These include single points, empty text paths, and unpainted object (no fill or stroke color). **[FIG. 4.8]**

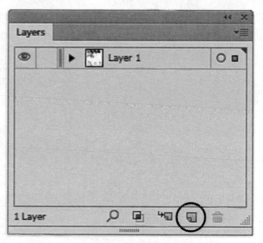

FIGURE 4.7   Create a new layer

FIGURE 4.8   The Clean Up tool

CHAPTER 5

Color, Gradients, and Patterns

Color can be applied to fills and strokes via the color panel, swatch panel, or by double clicking on the fill and stroke icons on the toolbar. **[FIG. 5.1]** There are four primary color modes in Illustrator—**RGB, CMYK, HSB,** and **grayscale**—as well as numerous color matching books.

   RGB stands for **red, green,** and **blue** and is intended for instances where light is projected to create the image (televisions, computer screens, smart phone screens, etc.). RGB uses specific levels of each component color (referred to as the R, G, and B channels) to create color. A value of 0 in each color channel will create black, a value of 255 in each will create white. **[FIG. 5.2]** **CMYK** stands for **cyan, magenta, yellow,** and **black** and is intended for instances where ink or dye will be deposited on some kind of surface (offset printing, desktop inkjet printers, etc.). CMYK uses a percentage of each component color to create all of the colors in an image. 0% of each color will not produce a color at all and will represent the color of the surface. **[FIG. 5.3, 5.4]** **HSB** stands for **hue, saturation,** and **brightness** and is intended for rendering and creating color entirely within a graphics program. Hue can be thought of as the color name (red, yellow, purple) and is represented by a degree of 0 to 360, representing the position on the color wheel. Saturation can be thought of as the variation of that particular color from very dull (gray) to very intense and is represented by a percentage from 0 to 100%. Brightness refers to the amount of white or black introduced into the color and is also represented by a percentage from 0 to 100%. **[FIG. 5.5]** **Grayscale** is a scale from white to black only and is represented as a percentage—0% is white and 100% is black. **[FIG. 5.6]** Colors can be edited in the expanded color panel (use **Show Options** in the context menu) and can be added to the swatch panel by clicking on the **New Color Swatch** icon. **[FIG. 5.7]** Any colors that are created for a particular Illustrator file are saved with that file.

FIGURE 5.1 The Default Illustrator colors (white fill and black stroke)

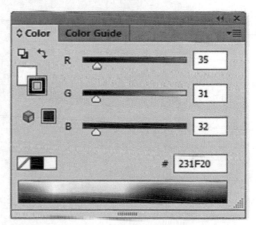

FIGURE 5.2 The RGB color mixing panel

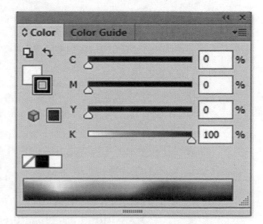

FIGURE 5.3 The CMYK color mixing panel

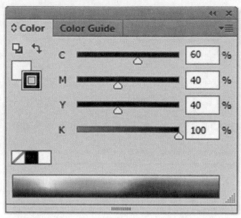

FIGURE 5.4 Mixing C, M, and Y colors with black produces a "rich Black." Varying the amount of each color makes warmer or cooler blacks as well. Keep the total amount of ink below 240%.

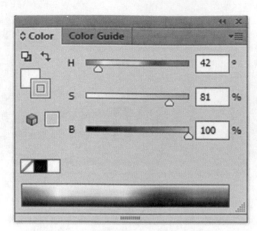

FIGURE 5.5 The HSB color mixing panel

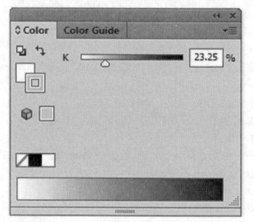

FIGURE 5.6 The Grayscale color mixing panel

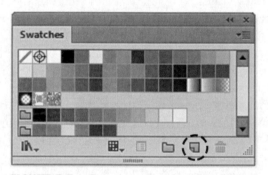

FIGURE 5.7 Create a new color swatch

Color Books (including Pantone and others) are a system of matching colors and maintaining consistency through a variety of mediums, including computer screens, various printers, textile mills, etc. There is a predefined formula for all the pantone colors, which makes picking and defining colors accurate. Libraries of swatches, including color books, are located under the WINDOW menu > SWATCH LIBRARIES or from within the swatch panel's context menu. To open swatches from a saved Illustrator file use the OTHER LIBRARY option.

A gradient is another type of swatch. It is fill that will place a color transition within an Illustrator shape or stroke. A gradient can transition between two or more colors and can either be linear (the transition happens along a straight path) or as radial (the transition starts at the center and radiates outward in concentric rings). [FIG. 5.8] Open the gradient editor by using the WINDOW menu > GRADIENT. [FIG. 5.9] A gradient is

FIGURE 5.8 Radial Gradient (above) and Linear Gradient (below)

defined by **color stops** (below the gradient preview) and **transition stops** (above the gradient preview). The color stops define the color and location within the gradient. The transitions define at what percentage between two colors the transition happens. Each of these stops can be moved around by dragging along the gradient preview or by selecting them and typing a number within the location area. Color stops can also be defined as having a percentage of opacity (100% is fully opaque). Gradients can be further defined as linear or radial within the gradient editor. To add a new color stop click below the gradient preview; double click on the gradient stop itself to define a new color either through the color mixing panel or the swatch panel. Delete a color stop by dragging it down and away from the preview window. The gradient panel window can be stretched out as wide as your monitor to define a gradient with many stops. To save a gradient after editing, click the **Add New Swatch** icon on the color panel.

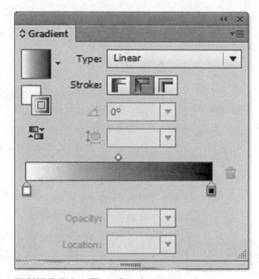

FIGURE 5.9   The Gradient panel

With a gradient applied to a shape, the **Gradient** tool (located on the toolbar) **[FIG. 5.10]** can be used to refine the gradient by changing the placement of stops and transitions, adding or deleting stops, or changing the axis of the gradient. The tool interacts directly with the gradient and will update the definition of the saved gradient.

FIGURE 5.10   Use the Gradient tool to make adjustments to gradient fills.

A gradient may also be applied to strokes and can be defined as either simply filling the stroke, following along the stroke from beginning to end, or moving across the stroke. **[FIG. 5.11]**

A **Pattern swatch** is a group of Illustrator shapes and lines that create a repeatable pattern. **[FIG. 5.12]** To create a pattern swatch, select a group of objects and drag them into the swatches panel. Illustrator considers the overall size of the selected objects as the boundary of the pattern swatch; all objects in the pattern will butt up next to itself as it is repeated.

FIGURE 5.11   Gradients used for strokes. Gradient within the stroke (left), along the stroke (middle), across the stroke (right).

FIGURE 5.12   Examples of Patterns swatches

There are a few rules to keep in mind for creating a tile that repeats seamlessly in two directions:

- Use the grid and snap to grid features to construct the tile. Work within a defined size (1″ × 1″ for instance) in order to control the placement of shapes.
- Use the Selection tool (black arrow) as the Move Transformation tool by selecting objects you want to copy and double clicking the black arrow icon. Using this tool will allow you to type in absolute measurements to copy objects from one side of the tile to the other.
- Remember: Whatever happens on one side of the tile must be completed on the other side.
- A pattern swatch may not be used as a fill or stroke within any shapes that will be used to make a new pattern swatch.
- If a shape is used to define a background color, change the stroke to none so no visible seams will be present in the swatch.
- Create an unpainted rectangle first to define the area of the repeated tile (this needs to be the bottom-most object).

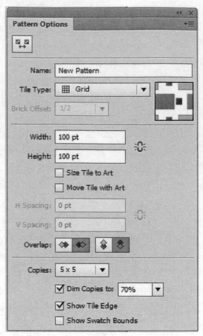

FIGURE 5.13 The Pattern Maker tool

Use the OBJECT menu > PATTERN > MAKE to utilize the **Pattern Maker** feature. **[FIG. 5.13]** The Pattern Maker will go into a special pattern editing space and the blank pattern will be automatically **added to the swatch panel**. The pattern tiles can be set up as a **Grid, Bricks by Row, Bricks by Column, Hexagons by Row,** and **Hexagons by Column.** These can be changed anytime during the editing process. The default size is 100 pts x 100 pts and can be changed to any size. To create a tiling pattern, begin by drawing or copying content within the Tile area. The Pattern Maker will provide a live preview. **[FIG. 5.14]** Overlapping of tile elements can be controlled by either having the **left or right side go in front** as well as the **top or bottom.** Click Done to save the tile into the swatches panel; **double clicking** the new tile in the swatch panel will bring up the pattern maker.

Use the Eyedropper tool **[FIG. 5.15]** to apply the same stroke, stroke width, and fill colors from one object to another. Select the object you want to apply the changes to, select the Eyedropper tool from the toolbar, and click on the object you want to take colors, stroke, or stroke width from.

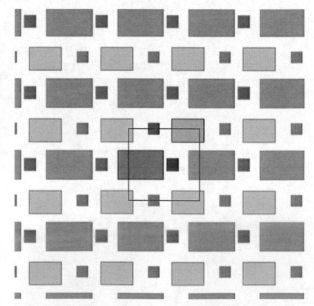

FIGURE 5.14 Live preview of Pattern maker

FIGURE 5.15 The Eyedropper tool

CHAPTER 6

ILLUSTRATOR BRUSHES

Brushes are used to apply a style along a path. There are four brushes that can be made in Illustrator; the **calligraphy** brush, the **scatter** brush, the **art** brush, and the **pattern** brush. [FIG. 6.1] Lines with brushes applied to them can be edited with the direct selection tool and the brush style will update along with it. Brushes may be accessed from the WINDOW menu > BRUSHES. [FIG. 6.2]

The **calligraphy** brush settings include **angle, roundness,** and **diameter.** All these can be set to have a **fixed size** or can have a **randomness** attribute added to change throughout any line segment. [FIG. 6.3]

The **scatter brush** takes Illustrator objects and scatters them along a line segment. Settings include **size, spacing, scatter,** and **rotation.** All these settings can be **fixed** or defined as **random.** When using random as the setting, a range must be provided for the randomness by defining two percentages. To create a

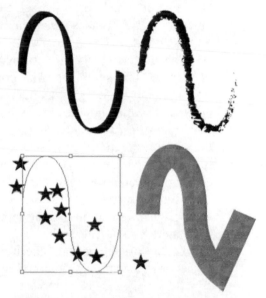

FIGURE 6.1 Calligraphy brush (above left), Art brush (above right), Scatter brush (below left), Pattern brush (below right)

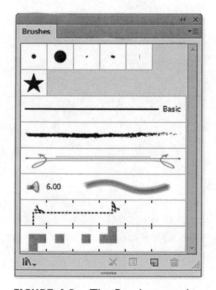

FIGURE 6.2 The Brushes panel

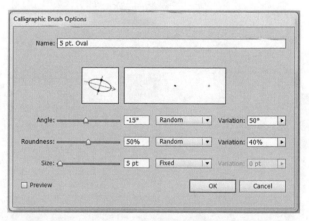

FIGURE 6.3 Calligraphy brush setting—Random will vary the particular setting throughout the brush stroke, and Fixed will keep the setting fixed at that setting.

scatter brush, drag the selected Illustrator objects into the brushes panel and define it as a scatter brush. **[FIG. 6.4]**

The **art brush** takes one object and stretches it along a path. Settings include the direction along the path, the scale of the object, whether the object maintains its proportions as the line segment grows, and how the object gets flipped along the path. A colorization method is also included in the **art brush options** box, this setting allows the brush to take on color other than the color used for the brush components. To create an art brush, drag the selected Illustrator objects into the brushes panel and define it as an art brush. **[FIG. 6.5]**

The **pattern brush** uses swatch objects as portions of line segments. The portions of the line segments (referred to as tiles) include **start caps, end caps, inside corners, outside corners,** and **sides.** When creating tiles for a pattern brush, consideration has to be given to how the tiles line up so that they appear seamless. Consideration also must be given to make sure that the overall height of one tile is not greater than any of the others. Illustrator, by default, will center tiles on a line segment directly at the horizontal midpoint. If the heights of your tiles are different and they need to be aligned, use an invisible shape that is the same height and in the same orientation for all tiles in the pattern brush. **[FIG. 6.6]**

The art brush and the pattern brush have the ability to warp and bend your tiles. Square-shaped objects wrapped along a curved line segment will get distorted.

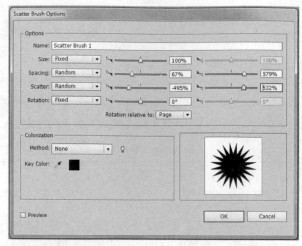

FIGURE 6.4   Scatter brush settings—Size refers to the overall size of the brush mark; spacing is the amount of space between instances of the mark; and scatter is the distance from the path. For a random setting, provide an upper and lower amount for variation.

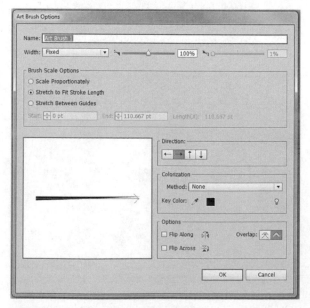

FIGURE 6.5   Art brush settings

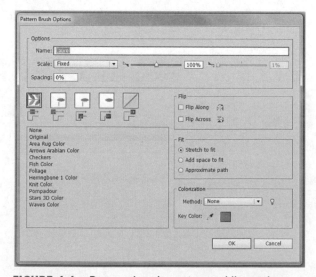

FIGURE 6.6   Pattern brush settings—All saved pattern swatches can be used as Pattern brush tiles.

CHAPTER 7

Compound Paths and Clipping Masks

A compound path is two or more paths that act as one path. If a compound path has a gradient or a pattern fill, the fill will go from one object to the next as if it is the same shape. Objects that are simply grouped, however, will have these properties applied to each individually. **[FIG. 7.1]** To create a compound path, select two or more closed path objects and go to the OBJECT menu > COMPOUND PATH > MAKE. If one object resides inside of another, the result will be as if the shape is a donut. **[FIG. 7.2]** To release the compound path back into its original components, use the OBJECT menu > COMPOUND PATH > RELEASE.

A clipping mask is a way of taking multiple objects, patterns, blends, or photographs and cropping them into a distinct shape. A clipping mask can be made from any closed Illustrator path and must be the object in front of the objects it is clipping; a compound path may be used as well. **[FIG. 7.3]** To create a clipping mask, select the objects, patterns, blends, or photographs as well as the clipping mask object and go to the OBJECT menu > CLIPPING MASK > MAKE. The

FIGURE 7.1 Two objects grouped together with gradient applied (above); a compound path comprised of the two objects with gradient applied (below).

FIGURE 7.2 A donut shape is created using compound paths.

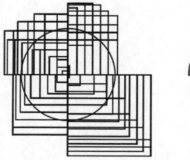

FIGURE 7.3 The collection of shapes with a circular shape to be used as a clipping mask (left); the resulting clipping mask (right).

shape of the clipping mask can be edited with the **Direct Selection** tool (white arrow). The contents of the clipping mask can be edited by going to the OBJECT menu > CLIPPING MASK > EDIT CONTENTS. To release the clipping mask go to the OBJECT menu > CLIPPING MASK > RELEASE MASK.

CHAPTER 8

Effects and the Appearances Panel

A variety of effects are included in the EFFECTS menu that will change vector shapes as well as images. The **distort and transform** effects modify existing shapes by either adding or moving points and line segments in a selected illustrator object. All effects are applied as a style, which means they can be modified later or removed. **Free Distort** places a four-sided bounding box around selected objects that can have each corner moved independently of the others. **[FIG. 8.1]** Pucker and Bloat either takes existing anchor points and moves them away from the center while pushing line segments into the center (pucker) or moves anchor points towards the center while pushing line segments away from the center (bloat). **[FIG. 8.2]** **Roughen** adds anchor points to a shape. Size refers to the scale to which the roughening takes place to line segments, and detail refers to how many new points are added on a per inch basis. Points can either be changed to smooth (curve points) or corners. **[FIG. 8.3]** **Transform** allows the use of all transformation tools (move, scale, rotate, reflect, and shear) as an

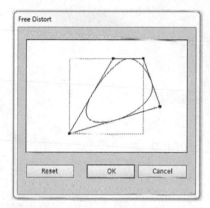

FIGURE 8.1   The Free Distort effect

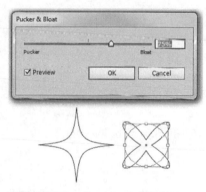

FIGURE 8.2   Pucker (left) & Bloat (right) effects

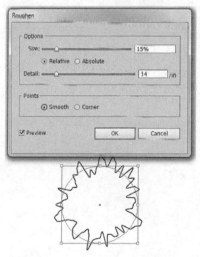

FIGURE 8.3   The Roughen effect

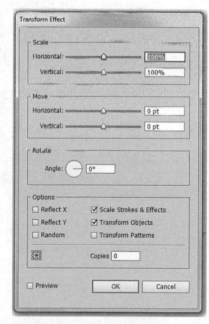

FIGURE 8.4   The Transform effect—all transformations can be applied as effects

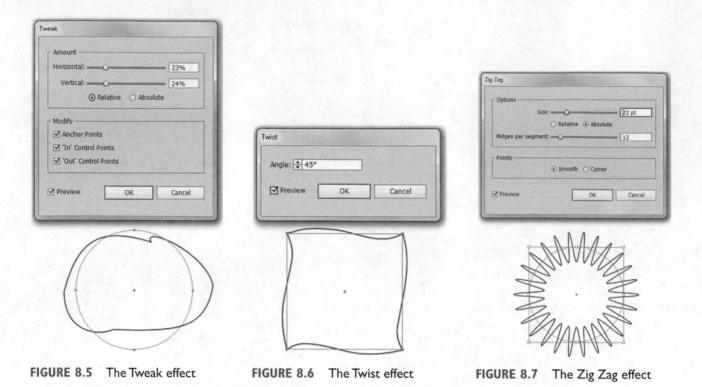

FIGURE 8.5 The Tweak effect   **FIGURE 8.6** The Twist effect   **FIGURE 8.7** The Zig Zag effect

effect, and any or all transformation may be applied. **[FIG. 8.4] Tweak** modifies existing anchor points and line segments without adding any new points. Tweak can modify the shape of line segments and positions of anchors either horizontally, vertically, or both. They can be tweaked relative to the page or the absolute size of the selected object. Further controls allows the inclusion or exclusion of anchor points "in" control points (handles on the side of line segments coming into the anchor point) or "out" control points (handles on the side of line segments leaving the anchor point). **[FIG. 8.5] Twist** rotates the anchor points of a selected object and forces line segments to become curved lines (if they are not already) and twist along with the shape. **[FIG. 8.6] Zig Zag** adds equal numbers of points (ridges) between line segments and moves them each a specified distance (size) in either direction from their original location. Points can be defined as smooth or corner, and the size can be relative to the page or absolute to the selection. **[FIG. 8.7]**

Once an effect has been applied to a shape it can be further modified by clicking the effect in the appearances panel [FIG. 8.8]. The appearances panel also includes all style applied to an object including stroke weights, stroke color, dashed lines, and fills. Within the appearances panel, multiple strokes may be applied to an object of varying weights as well as multiple fills. [FIG. 8.8A, 8.8B] Effects can be applied to an entire object or just to individual fills or strokes. Appearances can be saved for later use by saving them to the **Graphic Style panel. [FIG. 8.9]** Either select the object with the style and effects applied to it and click the **New Graphic Style** icon, or drag an object with a style applied to it into a free space within the panel.

FIGURE 8.9   The Graphic Styles panel, which is used to save appearances.

FIGURE 8.8B   An appearance with two fills and transformation effects applied to each fill individually.

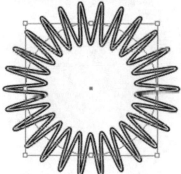

FIGURE 8.8A   An appearance with two strokes applied—the large weight is listed below the smaller weight to make the white line appear on top of the black.

CHAPTER 9

Blends

Blends are used for transitioning from one shape to another. Blends can work with open or closed paths, as well as grouped objects. Blends will also transition between colors used as the strokes and fills. **[FIG. 9.1]** To make a blend select at least two objects and go to the OBJECT menu > BLEND > MAKE. To adjust the number of transition objects that make up the blend, select the blend (which is now grouped together) and go to the OBJECT > menu > BLEND > BLEND OPTIONS. **[FIG. 9.2]** Blend options include either smooth color—useful for transitions between two objects with different color fills and no stroke; specific number of steps or space between the steps—useful for using two open paths to create a series of lines; and the orientation of the shape to the spine—either using the original orientation or perpendicular to the spine. The blend draws a path between the two objects; this is referred to as the blend spine and is an open Illustrator path. Points can be added to the path or so that the blend will follow a new path and not the default straight line. Another way to change the blend spine is to draw an open path and select both the open path and the blend and go to the OBJECT menu > BLEND > REPLACE SPINE. **[FIG. 9.3]** The new open path is now the spine for the blend. Original blend objects (shape, stroke, fill) can be updated and the blend will update according to those changes.

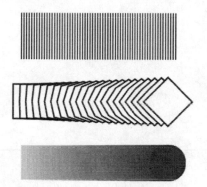

FIGURE 9.1 Blends between open paths, closed paths, and filled shapes

FIGURE 9.2 The Blend Options window

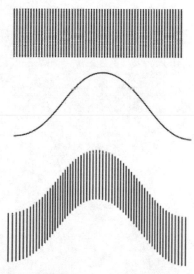

FIGURE 9.3 Original blend (top), new spine (middle), and new spine applied to blend (below).

27

CHAPTER 10

Type

Type is used throughout the Adobe Creative Suite. This chapter will address the specific uses of type within Illustrator. The section regarding InDesign will discuss typographic tools in detail.

Type can be placed into Illustrator in four ways. 1.) A string of text can be started by simply clicking in the drawing window with the type tool. **[FIG. 10.1A]** 2.) The type tool can be used to define a rectangular area in which to place type. The size of the rectangular frame can be adjusted and the text will reflow inside the area. **[FIG. 10.1B]** 3.) Type can be placed within any closed path by clicking on the inside of the shape with the type tool. **[FIG. 10.1C]** 4.) Type can be set along a path by clicking on any open or closed path with the type tool. **[FIG. 10.1D]**

Type in all of these instances can be edited and adjusted by using the Type tool and highlighting letters, words, sentences, or paragraphs in the same manner as a word processing program.

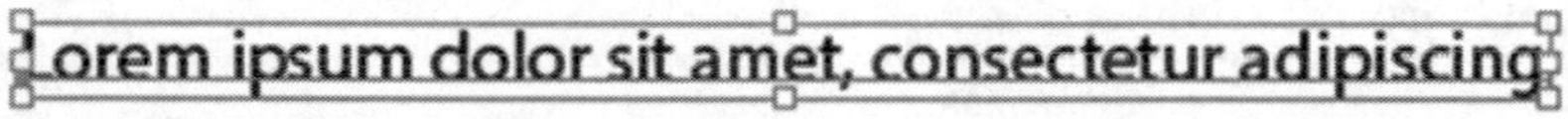

Lorem ipsum dolor sit amet, consectetur adipiscing

FIGURE 10.1A Default type path

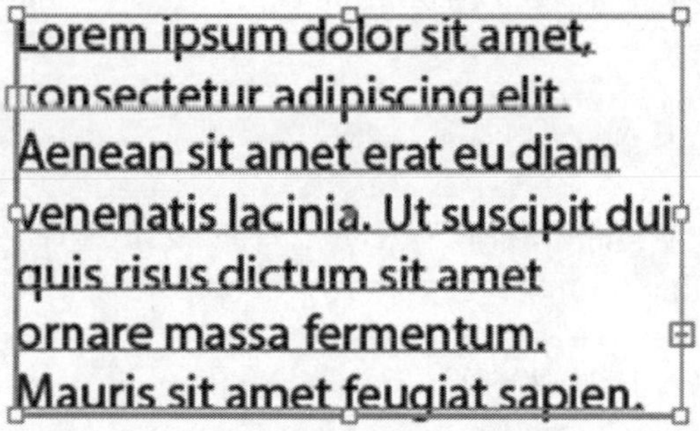

Lorem ipsum dolor sit amet,
consectetur adipiscing elit.
Aenean sit amet erat eu diam
venenatis lacinia. Ut suscipit dui
quis risus dictum sit amet
ornare massa fermentum.
Mauris sit amet feugiat sapien.

FIGURE 10.1B Type within a rectangular frame

Lorem ipsum
dolor sit amet,
consectetur adipiscing
elit. Aenean sit amet
erat eu diam venenatis
lacinia. Ut suscipit
dui quis risus

FIGURE 10.1C Area type

Lorem ipsum dolor sit amet, consectetur

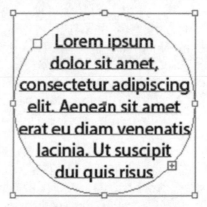

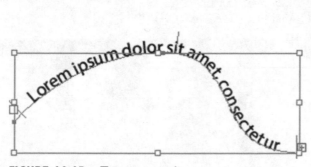

FIGURE 10.1D Type on a path

Adjustments that can be made to the type include: changing the typeface, style of the chosen typeface (bold, italic, etc., if available), size, leading (the space between lines of text), kerning (the space between pairs of letters), tracking (spacing between the letters in entire words, sentences, or paragraphs), vertical scale (letter width remains the same while the height changes), horizontal scale (character height remains the same while width changes), the baseline shift (how much above or below the originating text baseline), and rotation. All of these adjustments reside in the character panel (WINDOW menu > TYPE > CHARACTER or cmd/ctrl + T). **[FIG. 10.2]** The fill and stroke color can be changed for type as well.

For Type on a Path—To change where the type begins, use the white arrow and move the vertical blue line at the beginning of the line of type along the path. Moving the perpendicular line in the middle of the type to below the path will flip the type upside down and start it from the opposite direction. **[FIG. 10.3]** Type along a path may also be adjusted by going to the TYPE menu > TYPE ON A PATH. The relationship of type to the path can be changed from its default of rainbow (all of the letters sit perpendicular to the path) to skew (characters are skewed to stand vertically), 3D ribbon (characters are skewed and rotated to appear as if it's in 3D), stair step (characters stand vertically but are not skewed), or gravity (makes the characters appear as if effected by gravity by rotating and skewing). Further adjustments to type on a path can be found in the TYPE menu > TYPE ON A PATH > TYPE ON A PATH OPTIONS. **[FIG. 10.4]** The adjustments include the alignment of the type to the original path—either the ascenders (the character elements that ascend above the characters such as h, d, b), the descenders (the character elements that descend below the baseline such as p, q, j), the horizontal center of the type, or the baseline (bottoms of the characters).

Type can be converted to Illustrator objects using the TYPE menu > CREATE OUTLINES tool. This will take away any type editing adjustments but will allow the letter shapes to be edited using the direct selection tool, pathfinder tools, or effects. **[FIG. 10.5]** To convert to outlines, the type must be selected with the Selection tool (black arrow). Converted type can be used as a clipping mask (all elements must be a compound path).

FIGURE 10.2   The Character panel

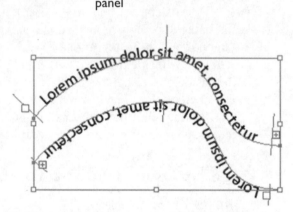

FIGURE 10.3   Type reversed on a path by dragging the vertical line in the middle of the type to below the path

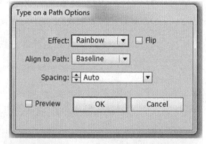

FIGURE 10.4   Type on a Path Options

FIGURE 10.5   Convert type to outlines to modify anchor points in the shape of the characters

SECTION 2

Photoshop

CHAPTER 11

Basic Navigation

Photoshop is a software tool that allows for the creation and manipulation of digital images. Although Photoshop can make original artwork similar to Illustrator, one of its core strengths is the ability to modify and create compositions with existing digital photography. Images in Photoshop are composed of a grid of pixels. **[FIG. 11.1]** Each pixel holds exactly one color and, when seen from a distance with its neighboring pixels, it makes up all of the colors and tonalities within an image. Editing in Photoshop requires changes to these individual pixels as opposed to editing in Illustrator, which meant changing the location of anchor points.

The Photoshop window consists of three main areas—the Menu (at the top of the screen), the Toolbar (typically on the left hand side), and the Panels (typically on the right or accessible from the WINDOW menu). **[FIG. 11.2]**

FIGURE 11.1 Images in Photoshop are referred to as "raster graphics" and are comprised of a grid of pixels.

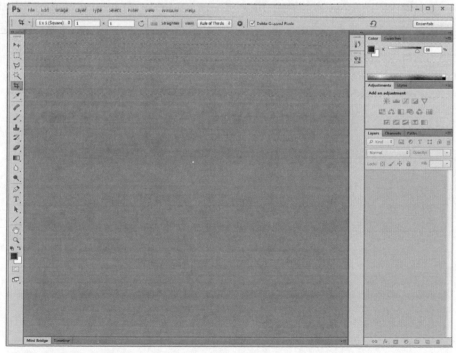

FIGURE 11.2 The Photoshop work area. The menu is at the top, the toolbar is on the left, and panels are located on the right.

CREATING A NEW FILE

To make a new file, go to the FILE menu > NEW. **[FIG. 11.3]** Select either a predefined size (preset) or type in custom dimensions for your file. The dimensions can be in many units of measurements including pixels, points, inches, or centimeters. Because Photoshop uses a grid of pixels to make up the image, a density of how many pixels per inch (PPI) must be selected. The default resolution is 72 PPI, which represents the maximum information that typical monitors can display—also referred to as screen resolution. Higher resolutions pack more information per square inch, a resolution of 300 PPI is typically used for printing (also referred to as high-res). Select a color mode: RGB—for images that will appear on a monitor, projector, or other device that emits light; CMYK—for images that will eventually be printed on some kind of surface; Grayscale—a strictly black and white mode with 256 levels of gray; Bitmap—a color mode in which pixels are either on (black) or off (white); or LAB—a more technical color space. Click OK.

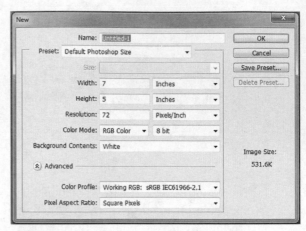

FIGURE 11.3 The New File window

General navigation. To zoom in, either use the magnifying glass **[FIG. 11.4]** and click on the image, or draw a square with the magnifying glass to zoom into a defined area. Hold the Option key (MAC) or the Alt key (PC) to zoom out with the magnifying glass. You can also use the VIEW menu > ZOOM IN, or VIEW menu > ZOOM OUT. VIEW menu > FIT ON SCREEN will resize the image to allow you see the entire image. VIEW menu > ACTUAL PIXELS will zoom into the actual size of the image (100%).

FIGURE 11.4 The Zoom tool

Many tools have other tools associated with them—these options are represented by a little black triangle on the bottom right corner of the icon. Press and hold the mouse button to access them.

At the bottom of the toolbar are Photoshop's foreground and background colors. **[FIG. 11.5]** As a default, black is used for the foreground and white is used for the background.

Type D to get to defaults.

Type X to swap the foreground and background colors or use the Rounded Arrow icon.

FIGURE 11.5 The default Photoshop colors: (black foreground, white background)

CHAPTER 12

Making Marks

Brushes are the tools for creating and editing discrete areas within Photoshop. Although this chapter deals with just the Brush tool, all of the methods for using and modifying this tool are shared with many others within the program. The Brush tool is found on the toolbar and is represented by an icon of a brush. [FIG. 12.1]

When the brush is selected, the options panel below the menu changes to introduce options for the brush. Clicking on the brush drop-down will present areas to set the brush size, the hardness of the brush (softer-edged brushes will have a hardness below 100%), and a library of brushes to choose from. [FIG. 12.2] Other options include the opacity (100% = full opacity anything below is considered transparent), and the painting mode (how the color chosen will mix with other colors already on the screen—to be discussed in later chapters). Further options control how a brush will act if Photoshop is connected to a drawing tablet.

The brushes presets panel presents options for creating and/or modifying brushes. The brushes panel can be accessed from the icon on the options toolbar or from the WINDOW menu > BRUSHES. [FIG. 12.3] **Brush Tip Shape** includes the size and hardness as well as the angle and roundness of the brush (to make a calligraphy-type brush) and spacing. When a brush creates a line, it repeats instances of its shape that overlap and making it appear as a continuous line. When spacing is set above 25% instances of the brush appear more discrete, and when over 100% the line will appear dotted. Further settings include: **shape dynamics**—angle, size, and roundness can be varied based on a jitter setting (a variation in percentage); **scattering**—how far away instances of the brush shape appear from the originating line as well as a multiple number of instances of the brush shape; **texture**—the use of a texture underlying the brush; **dual brush**—a secondary brush that controls the overall appearance of the original brush; **color dynamics**—controls for varying the hue, saturation, and brightness of selected colors; and **transfer**—controls variation in opacity and flow of each instance of the brush. Settings for adding **noise,** the appearance of **wet edges, building-up** effects, and **smoothing** the brush stroke are also available in the brush preset panel. Any changes made to the brush can be saved by clicking on make new brush preset from the brush panel context menu.

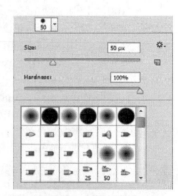

FIGURE 12.1 The Brush tool

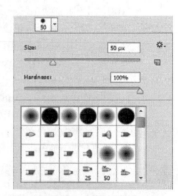

FIGURE 12.2 Brush presets—includes size, hardness of the brush, and a library of brush shapes

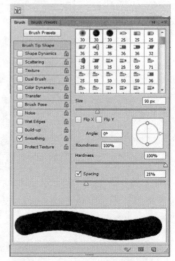

FIGURE 12.3 The Brushes panel includes extensive options for customizing brush shapes

The Pencil tool **[FIG. 12.4]** uses all of the same settings for the brushes except it will only create lines that have the pixels either turned on or off like a bitmap—there will be no smooth transition of color.

The Eraser tool **[FIG. 12.5]** has three modes for erasing—pencil, paint brush, and block. **[FIG. 12.6]** These modes will erase using the different brush styles, including opacity. The block eraser is a square shape that remains the same size relative to the monitor no matter how far you zoom in or out. The other erasers stay the same size relative to the file itself. The eraser will always erase to the background color unless there is more than one layer in a file.

To create a custom-shaped brush, make some marks or use an existing image and draw the rectangular marquee around the desired area. Go to the EDIT menu > DEFINE BRUSH PRESET **[FIG. 12.7]** and name the brush if preferred; the brush will now be in the brush library and can be modified with the brush panel. The brush preset can only use an area defined with a rectangle and will only use black and white information although color can be used as a source.

To delete everything from the screen, use the SELECT menu > ALL or cmd/cntl + A to select everything and then hit the DELETE key; the FILL window will pop up; choose a background color or white as the fill. Go to the SELECT menu > DESELECT or cmd/cntl + D to end the selection.

FIGURE 12.4 The Brush tool, Pencil tool, and associated tools

FIGURE 12.5 The Eraser tool

FIGURE 12.6 The Eraser tool options

FIGURE 12.7 Defining a Brush shape

CHAPTER 13

Simple Selections

Creating a selection means defining an area that is to be edited or modified while preserving other areas of the image. **Selections are an essential and core tool for Photoshop.** There are numerous methods to creating a selection, starting at less precise general area selections, to highly precise selections based on the shapes, color, and tones in a photograph. When a selection is created, Photoshop draws a blinking dotted line around the area selected; this is referred to as a **marquee** (or sometimes as marching ants). **[FIG. 13.1]**

FIGURE 13.1   An Elliptical selection

The most basic way to draw a selection is to use the **Marquee tools;** these are located on the upper left of the toolbar. They include a **rectangular selection,** an **elliptical selection,** and **single columns** or **rows** of pixels. **[FIG. 13.2]** To use these tools, choose the icon for the Marquee tool (hold down the mouse button to access the other options) and click and drag on the screen to define the size. Marquee selections can be further refined by adding or subtracting to the selection. Choosing a Marquee tool and then holding down the **Shift key** will allow you to **add** the new shape to the selection; holding down the **Opt/alt key** will **subtract** the shape from the selection. These can be used with any combination of marquee tools (rectangular, elliptical, single rows, more complex selections, etc.). **[FIG. 13.3]** The action of adding, subtracting, and creating a selection from an intersection of selections can also be chosen on the options panel. The **feather option** on the option panels controls the edges of selections and is defined in pixels (0px is a hard edge; anything above creates a softer edge to the selection). Feathering is available for all tools that create a selection; feathered edges and crisp edges can be combined. **[FIG. 13.4]**

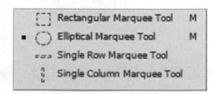

FIGURE 13.2   Marquee tools

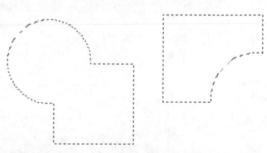

FIGURE 13.3   Adding and subtracting selections

The **Lasso tool** provides a method for making somewhat more precise selection. The choices include a **freehand** lasso, a **polygonal** lasso, and a **magnetic** lasso. The freehand lasso

FIGURE 13.4   Selection options

provides for a rough outline of an area. It is not incredibly precise, but can be refined by adding or subtracting selections from it, exactly the same way used with the marquee. **[FIG. 13.5]** To close the selection for the freehand lasso, either move the mouse back to the starting position or let go of the mouse (in this instance Photoshop will draw a line between the start and end point). The polygonal lasso is used to make a selection with line segments—use the mouse to click points around the area to be selected, and Photoshop will draw lines in between each mouse click. To close the polygon lasso, either click back on the starting point or double click on the screen. **[FIG. 13.6]** The magnetic lasso is used to make selections based on areas of contrast identified in a photograph. The magnetic lasso works well with images that have strong contrast between foreground and background areas. Feathered selections can be used for all the lassos.

With all selections, the option of anti-aliased can be checked or unchecked. Anti-aliased means that Photoshop will create a selection that appears smooth (it will use a combination of solid and transparent pixels to do this). Unchecking this option makes a more jagged selection.

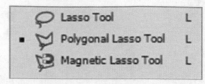

FIGURE 13.5   Lasso tools

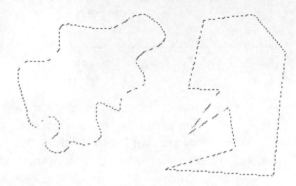

FIGURE 13.6   Hand-drawn and Polygon Lassos

CHAPTER 14

Selections Based on Color

To create a selection based on a limited area of color, use the **Magic Wand** tool (associated with the Quick Selection tool). **[FIG. 14.1]** The magic wand samples a chosen color and then create a selection based on that sample and similar areas of color. **[FIG. 14.2]** The options for the magic wand include tolerance, contiguous, anti-aliased, and use all layers. **Tolerance** refers to how close an adjacent color needs to be to be included in the selection. This can be set from 1 to 255, where 255 will select the entire image, and lower values (the default is 32) will sample clusters of similar colors. **Contiguous** means that the colors do not have to be adjacent to one another, and Photoshop will sample from the entire image. **Anti-aliased** determines whether the selection will have transparent or jagged edges. When **use all layers** is selected, the wand will sample from the entire image, not just the current layer. Holding down the **Shift key** will provide additions to the selection, the **Cmd/cntl** key will provide subtractions; these may be combined with any other selection tools.

The **Quick Selection** tool provides a dynamic method of creating selections by analyzing the content of the image and identifying areas of contrast. The Quick Selection tool uses a round or oval-shaped brush to identify areas in the image that are closely associated by color and tonal value. The brush shape can be modified by size, hardness, spacing, and angle—the exact same settings available for the Brush tool. **[FIG. 14.3]** To create a selection, begin by dragging the cursor through areas of the foreground that are consistent in color or value. If the tool selects areas of the background, choose the **Subtract from** selection tool from the option panel (or hold Opt or Alt) to select in the unwanted areas. Generally there will be some back and forth to generate the desired results. **[FIG. 14.4]**

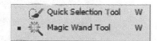

FIGURE 14.1 Quick Selection and Magic Wand tools

FIGURE 14.2 Magic Wand selection—makes a selection based on a sampled area of color

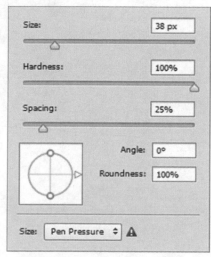

FIGURE 14.3 Quick Selection "Brush" settings

FIGURE 14.4 With a selection made with the Quick Selection tool, Photoshop analyzes color areas to create a more refined selection

FIGURE 14.5 Color Range selection builds a selection based on a selection of color/s

Use the SELECT menu > COLOR RANGE to create a selection based on a color in the image. Start by using the eyedropper tool to select a preferred area of color and then use the fuzziness slider to add a range of the sampled color; the range is between 0 and 200. [**FIG. 14.5**] Additional colors can be added by using the **Add to sample tool** or removed by using the **Subtract from sample** tool. If **localized color clusters** is selected, Color Range will only look for similar color within discrete areas of the images. The **range** setting can be adjusted to expand the location area. Color Range can also create selections based on a general hue (red, yellow, green, blues, cyan, or magenta) or a tonal property (highlights, midtones, or shadows). The selection that Color Range creates will be based on all the layers in the image.

CHAPTER 15

Refining Selections

As precise as some of the above-mentioned tools are in creating selections based on color, there will still need to be some hands-on editing to refine the selection. Photoshop uses an editing area referred to as an **Alpha Channel** to allow for adjustment using all of Photoshop's available tools.

Photoshop uses the term *channel* to define ways of viewing the components or the composite of color areas that make up an image. In an RGB image, there are Red, Green, and Blue **Component** channels, and an RGB **Composite** channel. An Alpha Channel is an additional, non-printing channel that is used to save selection information. **[FIG. 15.1]**

An Alpha Channel may be saved by first making a selection and then going to 1.) the SELECT menu > SAVE SELECTION (selections can be named or added to or subtracted from existing alpha channels.) **[FIG. 15.2]** or 2.) Clicking the **Save selection as channel** icon on the bottom of the **channels panel**. Clicking on the **new channel** icon at the bottom of the channels panel will create a blank alpha channel.

An alpha channel is a black and white view of a selection. Areas that are pure white represent the selected areas whereas black represents areas that are not selected. Areas that are any shade of gray are considered a partial selection—lighter tones allow more of an effect or editing to happen, and darker tones will allow less. **[FIG. 15.3]**

To view the channel, click on the **Visibility** icon for the alpha channel in the channels panel and turn off visibility for the composite channel; click on the name of the alpha channel as well to ensure editing happens in that channel. Once the channel is visible and editable, brush and eraser tools can be used to clean up areas. Turn on the **visibility** of the composite channel to see the image while making edits to the alpha channel. The alpha channel will now appear as a red mask over top the image. Areas of red

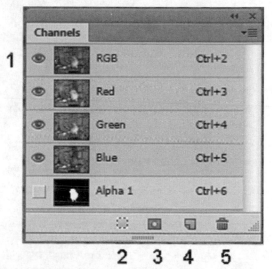

FIGURE 15.1 The Channels panel—1. Visibility Icon 2. Load Channel as a Selection 3. Save Selection as Channel 4. New Channel 5. Delete Channel

FIGURE 15.2 Save Selection window

FIGURE 15.3 A selection (above) and the resulting Alpha channel (below). White indicates a selected or editable area, black represents non-selected or masked.

FIGURE 15.4 A red and clear overlay represents the Alpha channel when the alpha channel is made visible along with the composite channel.

represent black (not-selected or masked) and clear areas represent white (selected). **[FIG. 15.4]** The color of the mask as well as its opacity can be adjusted by double clicking on the name of the alpha channel. **[FIG. 15.5]**

To activate a saved alpha channel, either 1.) select the channel by name in the channels palette and then select the icon for **Load channel as a selection** or 2.) go to the SELECT menu > LOAD SELECTION, choose the saved alpha channel, and click OK. Load selection can also use alpha channels from other open documents; can invert the channel; or can add, subtract, and intersect with existing selections. **[FIG. 15.6]**

A NOTE about INVERSE and INVERT. *Inverse in the selection menu means to make the opposite of the existing selection. Invert means to reverse the pixel information (i.e., change black to white and white to black).*

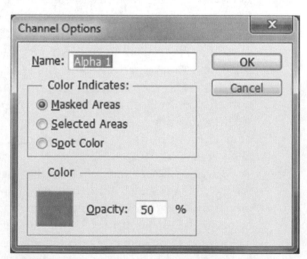

FIGURE 15.5 Channel options for how visible channels appear.

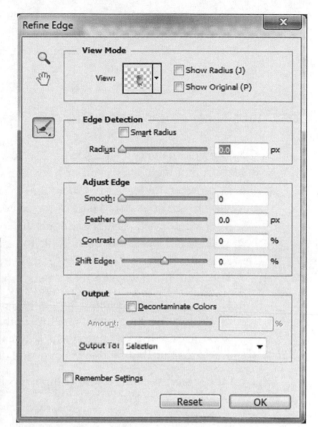

FIGURE 15.7   The Refine Edge window

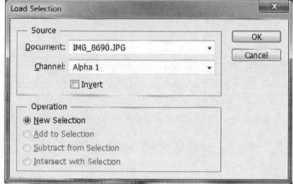

FIGURE 15.6   Load Selection window

The **refine edge panel** [FIG. 15.7] appears anytime a selection tool is being used. Refine edge provides adjustments for active selections. **View mode** provides seven different viewing options for the selection: Marching Ants (the marquee), Overlay (a quick mask type view), On Black (the selected part of the image with black filling in the masked area), On White (the selected part of the image with white filling in the masked area), Black and White (an alpha channel view of the selection), On Selection (the selected part of the image with transparent pixels filling in the masked area), and Reveal Layer (the entire unmodified image). **Edge detection** provides further refinement in detecting the edge of the selection especially if the edge is not clearly defined. Using smart radius allows Photoshop to make a qualified guess at the edges (especially good with thin areas of hair, etc.). **Adjust edges** modifies the selection edge by smoothing (getting rid of bumps and irregularities), feathering (softening the edges), contrast (modifying the soft edges of the selection), and shift edge (increasing or decreasing the overall size of the selection). **Output** tells Photoshop what to do with the selection once selected: Selection (creates a selection) layer mask (creates a mask associated with the layer), new layer (creates a new layer from the selection), or new document (make a new file from the selection). The **Decontaminate edges** option deletes color from the fringes of the selection.

The **Quick Mask** makes a temporary visible alpha channel from an active selection. To activate a quick mask, either type **Q** on the keyboard or select the **Edit in quick mask mode** icon at the bottom of the toolbar. [FIG. 15.8] Entering Quick Mask (or making an existing alpha channel visible) will reverse the default colors, making the background black and the foreground white. Painting with the brush will add to the selection; erasing (to the background color) will add to the mask or deselected areas. Painting with a shade of gray will produce a semi-transparent mask. To

FIGURE 15.8   The Quick Mask icon

ensure the default colors are present, type **D** on the keyboard. The Quick Mask appears temporarily as a channel in the channels palette and can be made into a permanent channel by dragging it to the New channel icon. The composite channel (RGB) can be temporarily turned off and the Quick Mask will appear as black and white.

SELECTIONS FROM COMPONENT CHANNELS

Component channels can also be used to make selections. The varying shades of gray will make a selection that includes partial or transparent selection information. Any shade of gray in the channel that is between middle gray (50%) and black (0%) will not be represented with a selection marquee, but will still be considered part of the selection.

Many times component channels are used to form the basis for a mask to extract a figure from a background. If this is the case, look for a channel that has the clearest definition and best contrast. Image adjustments as well as any editing tool may be used to refine the new alpha channel.

There are three ways to make a component channel a selection:

1. Drag the component channel to the New channel icon in order to make a new alpha channel.
2. Select the component channel in the channels palette (click on the name of the channel), then click the load selection as a Channel icon on the channels palette.
3. Hold the Cntl/cmd key down and click on the component channel name.

Turn the visibility icon for the composite channel on to view the channel as a mask.

CHAPTER 16

Vector-based Selections

Vector paths may be used as a method to create selections in Photoshop. The tool is similar to Illustrator's Pen tools but does not have the full range of abilities. Despite this, complex paths can be constructed. Vector paths are saved in the paths panel. [FIG. 16.1]

Paths are drawn on top of the image and will not interfere with the image below; it merely serves as an illustration of a selection. Paths can be moved with the **Path Selection tool,** reshaped as in Illustrator with a **Direction Selection** tool, [FIG. 16.2] and points can be added, subtracted, and converted into corner or straight points. [FIG. 16.3] When paths are first created, they will be temporarily named "Work Path" and will not be saved if a new path is created. Double click the name of the path thumbnail to rename the path and save it with the file.

Active selections can be converted into vector paths by clicking the **Convert selection to path** icon on the path panel. Vector paths can be converted to selections as well by clicking the **Convert to selection** icon. Further options for this conversion can be found by using the Convert to selection option under the **Path Panel Context Menu.**

Paths may be filled with the foreground color by clicking the **fill path** icon on the path panel. Further filling options are also found under the Path Panel Context Menu. Paths may be stroked with the current brush and foreground color by clicking the **stroke path.** Further stroke options are also found under the Path Panel Context Menu. Fills and strokes created using the methods presented **will not** be updated when the original path is adjusted. In order to achieve this, a vector-shaped layer will need to be created.

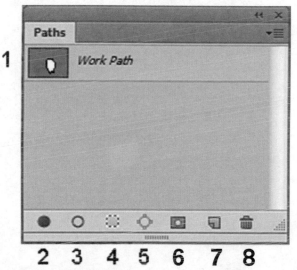

FIGURE 16.1 The Path panel—1. Active Path 2. Fill Path with Foreground Color 3. Stroke Path with Brush 4. Create Selection from Path 5. Create Path from Selection 6. Create Vector Mask 7. New path 8. Delete path

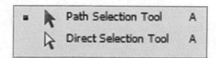

FIGURE 16.2 Path Selection and Direct Selection tools (black arrow and white arrow)

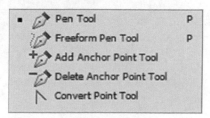

FIGURE 16.3 Pen tools

45

CHAPTER 17

Fills and Strokes

An area can be filled in two ways in Photoshop—the **Fill** tool or the **Paint Bucket.** The Fill command (EDIT menu > FILL or the DELETE key) creates a fill for either the entire image or a selected area. The Fill tool uses either the **foreground color,** the **background color, black, white, 50% gray, a custom color, pattern,** a saved moment in the images **history,** or **content-aware** (Photoshop will attempt to fill in the selection with a fill that represents areas around the selection). **[FIG. 17.1]** These fills can be modified to have an **opacity** percentage (between 1% and 100%) and can use various color mixing modes. The last option, **preserve transparency** determines whether the Fill command can fill in transparent or empty areas of layers.

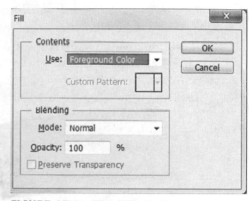

FIGURE 17.1   The Fill window

When pattern is chosen for the fill, a dropdown box will display a list of default patterns. **[FIG. 17.2]** Further patterns may be accessed from the CONTEXT menu (represented by a small gear). A custom pattern may be created as well by selecting a portion of an image and then going to the EDIT menu > DEFINE PATTERN. **[FIG. 17.3]** Any shaped selection can be used to produce the pattern; however, non-rectangular shapes will be made into a rectangle by using the overall proportions of the selected area and filling the rest in with white. The pattern will retain all of the color from the original selection.

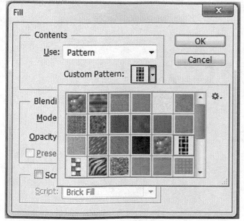

FIGURE 17.2   Fill using Pattern opens up the pattern library

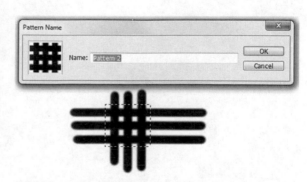

FIGURE 17.3   Defining a custom pattern

The **Paint bucket** tool, associated with the Gradient tool, [FIG. 17.4] can be used to fill in areas of the image as well as selected areas. Use the tool by clicking on an area in order to fill it with color or a pattern. If there are gaps in the boundary of the specified area (areas not defined with a selection), color or pattern will flood into adjacent spaces. Options for the paint bucket include whether the foreground color or a pattern is used to fill in areas, the opacity of the fill, and the type of color mixing mode. Further options include the **tolerance, anti alias, contiguous,** and **use all layers.** [FIG. 17.5]

The Stroke tool (EDIT menu > STROKE) [FIG. 17.6] uses a selection to create an outline. The options include the color (the default is the foreground color, but any color can be chosen by clicking on the color to get to the color picker window); the **location** of the stroke—either **inside, outside,** or the **center** of the selection; and the **color mode** and **opacity** settings.

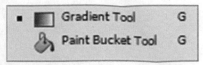

FIGURE 17.4   Gradient tool and Paint Bucket tool

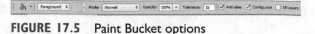

FIGURE 17.5   Paint Bucket options

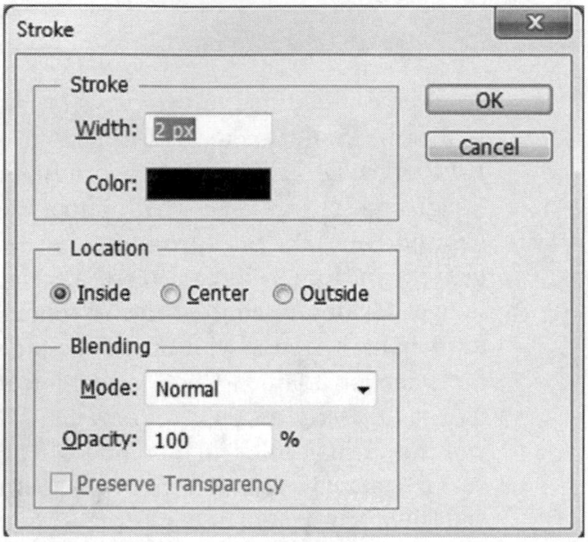

FIGURE 17.6   The Stroke window

CHAPTER 18

Layers

Layers are essential to using Photoshop as a composition tool. Layers provide the ability to float images on top of other images, change the opacity of those images, change the way those images interact with the image below it, and re-organize the images. The settings given to each layer can be constantly changed.

By default, new Photoshop files are created with one layer, the **Background Layer** (this appears in the layers panel as *background*). New layers may be added to an image by either 1.) clicking the **New layer** icon at the bottom of the layers panel; 2.) going to the LAYER menu > NEW > LAYER; 3.) dragging an existing layer to the **new layer** icon; or 4.) pasting content in from another file. New layers are **transparent**—meaning they have no background color—and will be able to have opacity and color mode settings applied to them. Transparency is represented by a gray and white checkerboard. Any layer may be deleted, including the background, by simply dragging the layer to the small Trash can icon (**delete layer**) in the layers panel. New layers can be renamed by **double clicking the name** in the layers panel. The background layer can be copied and/or renamed; if it is renamed it is now considered a transparent layer. **[FIG. 18.1]**

To move elements on a transparent layer, use Photoshop's **Move** tool to move the contents of the layer. There is no need to make a selection unless a specific area is to be singled out on the layer. Layers can have their **transparent pixels locked**—meaning if there is pixel information on the layer it can be edited but areas where there is no information cannot be edited. To lock all editing on a layer, select the **Lock image pixels** icon to lock the movement of elements on a layer, select the **Lock movement** icon. To lock all select the **Lock all** icon.

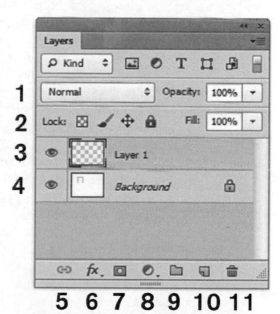

FIGURE 18.1 The Layer panel—1. Blending mode and Opacity 2. Locking different aspects of layers 3. A New Transparent Layer 4. Default Background Layer 5. Link Layers 6. Layer Effects 7. Layer Mask 8. Adjustment Layers 9. Layer Groups 10. New Layer 11. Delete Layer

LAYER MASKS

A **layer mask** is used to nondestructively hide content on a selected layer. The layer mask appears as a **black and white thumbnail** linked to the layer. **[FIG. 18.2]** Areas in the layer mask thumbnail that appear in white reveal areas of the layer, areas that are black hide or mask the layer. Levels of gray partially reveal the content—lighter shades reveal more, darker shades less. This operates on the same principal as alpha channels because the layer mask IS an alpha channel. A layer mask can be created by making a selection and then clicking the Layer mask icon, or a blank layer mask can be created from the Layer mask icon and then modified using standard editing tools (brush, pencil, eraser). To edit within the layer mask, select the layer mask thumbnail (brackets will appear around the thumbnail indicating it is active). The layer and the mask are **linked** by default, meaning that if the layer moves, the mask moves along with it. The layer can be separated from the mask by clicking the **Chain link** icon. By doing this, the layer content can be moved and the mask will stay in place, or the mask can be moved with the layer content staying in place, depending on whether the layer or mask thumbnail is selected. Options for deleting, permanently applying, or temporarily disabling the layer mask can be found under the LAYER menu > LAYER MASK.

ADJUSTMENT LAYERS

Adjustment layers are a method of non-destructively editing your image. **[FIG. 18.3]** Adjustments can be applied and then modified at any time. Any number or combinations of adjustments may be used. The adjustments include all of the tools found under the IMAGE menu > ADJUST-MENTS (see Chapter 22). Also included are solid color, gradient, and pattern adjustment layers. Each adjustment layer contains an Adjustment icon as well as a linked layer mask. By default, the mask is solid white (meaning the adjustment will take full effect over the canvas), but it can be modified using any editing tools and will appear in the channels panel when that adjustment layer is specified. By default, the adjustments will affect all of the layers below it; this can be limited to just the layer below by using **Clip to layer** icon in the adjustments panel. **[FIG. 18.4]**

FIGURE 18.2　An active Layer mask

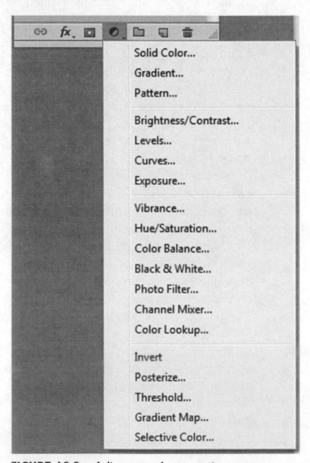

FIGURE 18.3　Adjustment Layer options

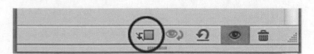

FIGURE 18.4　Limit effect of Adjustment Layer to layer below

LAYER EFFECTS

Layer effects produce a limited range of effects for individual layers—these include drop shadows, inner shadows, outer/inner glows, bevel and emboss, satin, color/gradient/pattern overlays, and strokes. **[FIG. 18.5]** Apply layer effects by clicking the **"fx"** icon on the layer panel. Layer effects will appear listed below layers in the panel with an individual listing for each effect. A Visibility icon will appear next to each effect. Layer effects can be modified at any time; **double click** the effect associated with the layer in order to make adjustments or change the effect entirely. Change the **fill percentage** to zero to show the effect with none of the layer information present. Effects may also be applied to blank layers in the layers panel, any new drawing/painting on the layer will automatically receive the effect. Layer effects can be applied to all types of layers including type, shapes, and smart objects.

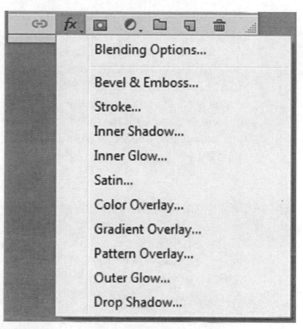

FIGURE 18.5 Layer Effects options

ORGANIZING LAYERS

Layers may be rearranged by dragging a layer above or below other layers in the layers panel. Use the layer group tool to make groups of layers in order to turn many layers on and off at once and apply transformations or effects to multiple layers at once. **[FIG. 18.6]** Drag individual layers (or multiple layers by using the Shift key) into the new group. Layers or layer groups can be renamed by double clicking the layer's name in the layer panel. This is a useful practice with compositions with many layers as it makes layers easy to find and identify quickly.

FIGURE 18.6 Grouped layers

SMART OBJECTS

Smart objects appear as layers that cannot be edited using standard editing tools, but can be transformed, modified with a layer mask, layer effects, filters, or adjustment layers. Smart object layers can also have their content replaced with content from another file. Smart objects can be created by using the FILE menu > PLACE command or by pasting in content from Illustrator or by defining a layer as a smart object (LAYER menu > SMART OBJECT > CONVERT TO SMART OBJECT). To replace the contents of a smart object, use the LAYER menu > SMART OBJECT > REPLACE CONTENT and then choose a new file. Any existing transformations, effects, or layer masks will be preserved. Any file type that can be opened in Photoshop can be used. To rasterize—meaning to be able to edit the file with standard editing tools—go to the LAYER menu > SMART OBJECT > RASTERIZE.

FLATTENING AND MERGING LAYERS

To flatten an image (take away all layer info), go to the LAYER menu > FLATTEN IMAGE. To merge select layers go to the LAYER menu > MERGE DOWN (to merge the top most selected layer to the layer below) or go to the LAYER menu > MERGE VISIBLE to merge all visible layers.

CHAPTER 19

Vector Tools in Photoshop

Photoshop provides the ability to use **vector shapes** on a limited basis within the program. To create vector shapes select a **Shape** tool **[FIG. 19.1]** from the toolbar (rectangle, rounded rectangle, ellipse, polygon, line, or custom shapes), and either draw it out on the canvas freehand or click the tool on the screen to define the size as in Illustrator. **[FIG. 19.2]** Each individual shape will produce its own layer in the layer panel. **[FIG. 19.3]** Each vector shape can have the **fill** and **stroke** changed by selecting it with the **black arrow** and making adjustments in the **options bar.** Further stroke options include the **alignment** of the stroke (inside, centered, or outside), **caps** on the end of lines (butt, rounded or square), **corners** (miter, rounded, or beveled), plus the ability to create a custom **dashed line. [FIG. 19.4]** Use the **white arrow** (direct selection tool) to modify the vector shape (move points, adjust curve handles). The shape tools may also be used to create paths for selections (unfilled, unstroked) or create shapes comprised only of pixels with no vector information. **[FIG. 19.5]** Two or more shapes may be com-

FIGURE 19.1 Vector Shape tools

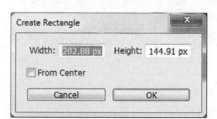

FIGURE 19.2 Vector Shapes can be created by clicking on the screen and typing dimensions

FIGURE 19.3 Vector Shape layers

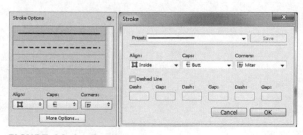

FIGURE 19.4 Stroke options

FIGURE 19.5 Vector Shape options

bined by using the **path operations** dropdown. Paths can also be subtracted as well as generate the intersection or exclusion area from more than one shape. **[FIG. 19.6]** The **Pen** tool may be used to create vector shapes as well.

When using the **Line** tool, a line weight has to be set for the overall **thickness** of the line. Further options include **arrowheads** on the start and end of the line as well as the width, height, and shape (concavity) of the arrowhead. These are accessed from the gear dropdown. **[FIG. 19.7]**

When using **custom shapes,** predefined vector shapes are used. These are located in the shape dropdown; further libraries of shapes can be found in the SHAPE CONTEXT menu. **[FIG. 19.8]**

Vector layers can have effects, adjustments, and layer masks applied to them. To rasterize a vector shape for further editing, go to the LAYER menu > RASTERIZE > SHAPE.

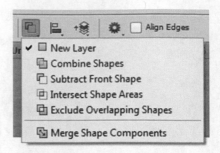

FIGURE 19.6   Vector Path Operations

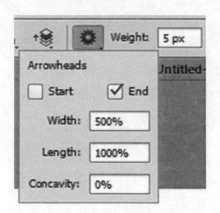

FIGURE 19.7   Vector Line options

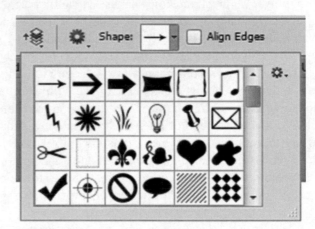

FIGURE 19.8   Custom Shape Library

CHAPTER 20

Transformations

As in Adobe Illustrator, Photoshop's transformations provide tools to manipulate the position, rotation, and distortion of selected pixels. Photoshop's transformations include **move, scale, rotate, skew, perspective, distort, warp,** and **reflection** options; these are found under the EDIT menu > TRANSFORM. When a transformation is chosen, a bounding box will be drawn around the extents of the selected parts of the image. **[FIG. 20.1]** The bounding box will include anchor points on all four corners and midpoints of each side, and a reference point for the center will be displayed as well. The reference point can be relocated using the cursor or can be selected as any of the four corners as well as the middle of each of the sides within the options toolbar. **[FIG. 20.2]**

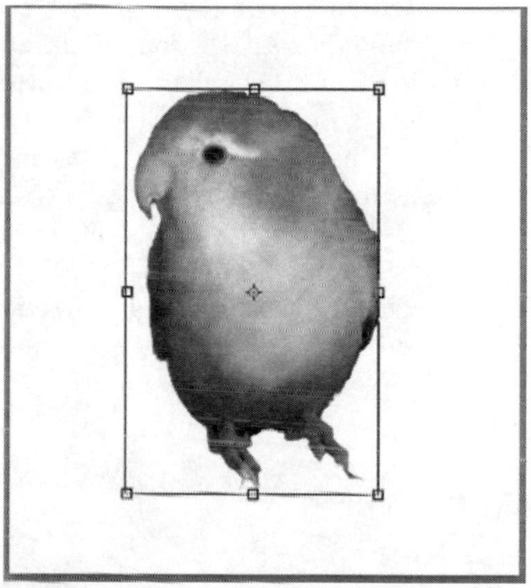

The **Move** tool (the black arrow at the top of the toolbar) is used to change the position of selected parts of the image.

Scale increases or decreases the overall size of a selected part of an image. By choosing the corner anchor in a transformation bounding box, the selection can be scaled in both the horizontal (H) or vertical (V) directions. By choosing to scale from one of the side anchors the selection will scale only in that direction. Hold the Shift key down to scale in proportion.

FIGURE 20.1   A Transformation Bounding Box

FIGURE 20.2   Transformation Controls

Rotate revolves the selected part of the image. When first selected, the reference point is in the center; the point may be moved by clicking and dragging to a new location. Hold the Shift key down to force the rotation into 15-degree intervals.

Skew slants the selected part of the image in either the horizontal direction, vertical direction, or both. Choose a midpoint anchor to initiate the transformation.

Perspective provides the illusion that the selected part of the image is receding back into space in a one- or two-point perspective. Dragging a corner anchor point will force the other corner (depending on the movement of the point, H or V) to mirror that movement.

Distort freely distorts the selected part of the image. Pull from any corner to make adjustments.

Warp places a grid overtop the selected part of the image and provides the ability to relocate each intersection of the grid as well as change the curvature of the sides of the grid via curve handles. **[FIG. 20.3]** Within the warp options are presets for various warps including arcs, arches, bulges, and a variety of other shapes. **[FIG. 20.4]**

The transformation option toolbar provides areas to numerically control most of the transformations (except perspective and distort).

To commit the transformation (make it permanent), either click the **check mark** on the options panel, hit the **Return** key on the keyboard, **double click** the transformation, or select a **new tool.** To cancel the transformation, either click the **cancel button** on the options toolbar or hit the **ESC key** on the keyboard. Transformations may be performed one after another before committing the transformation.

The EDIT > TRANSFORM menu provides shortcuts for common rotations (180°, 90° clockwise and 90° counter-clockwise) and reflections (flip horizontal, flip vertical).

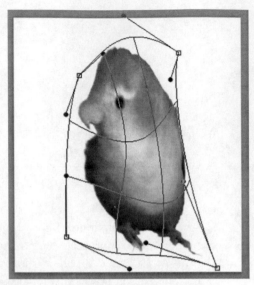

FIGURE 20.3 The Warp Transformation

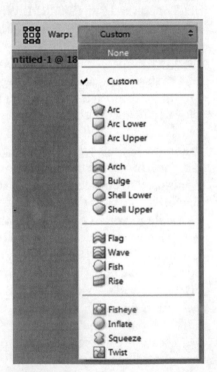

FIGURE 20.4 Warp presets

CHAPTER 21

Luminosity and Channels

Luminosity refers to the darkness or brightness of a particular area. In Photoshop, there are 256 levels of luminosity, measured on a scale from 0 to 255, where 0 represents pure black and 255 represents pure white; level 128 represents 50% gray.

The Histogram **[FIG. 21.1]** (found in the WINDOW menu > HISTOGRAM) is used to view a representation of the distribution of luminosity or tonal values within an image. The histogram displays a horizontal bar representing the full range of values (0 to 255). Above the bar are vertical lines representing how much information in the image is at each level; spikes in the histogram mean that there is a large concentration of tonal value at some location in an image (a very bright image, or one with a tremendous amount of highlights, for instance, would have a spike towards the higher end of the scale). The histogram can view this tonal distribution for the entire image, its individual channels, or strictly for the luminosity or brightness value. The histogram is used in some image adjustments.

Grayscale tonality is used throughout Photoshop, especially within the component channels of RGB images. Component channels (the individual R, G, and B channels) located in the channels panel represent the brightness of each component color in an image. RGB colors are expressed as a combination of three numbers (0,0,0 or 255, 255, 255, for instance) representing the individual level of luminosity in each channel. The resulting combination of all three component channels appears as the actual color within the composite channel (RGB).

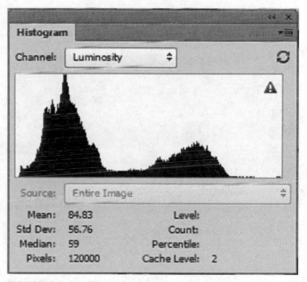

FIGURE 21.1 The Histogram window

The composite channel is the channel in which most editing takes place, but for image correction purposes, editing can also be performed within individual channels.

CHAPTER 22

Image Adjustments

The Adjustments section of the IMAGE menu contains many image correction and modification tools. Any of these tools can be used on the entire image or within selections.

The **Levels** tool **[FIG. 22.1]** is used to adjust the range of tones used in an image. In an RGB image, the Levels tool can be used in either the composite channel (RGB) or the component red, green, and blue channels. The top portion of the Levels tool is used to change the input levels. Three points within the luminosity scale (histogram) can be adjusted—the **black point** (the darkest area of the image, level 0), **gamma** (the mid-point between black and white), and the **white point** (the lightest area, level 255). By drag-

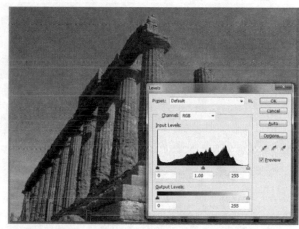

FIGURE 22.1 The Levels tool

ging the black point towards the middle, the darkest areas of the image are re-assigned. For instance, if the black point is relocated to level 123, everywhere in the image that is at level 123 and below will be considered pure black. The remaining tonal values throughout the image will be relocated to accommodate the adjustment. **[FIG. 22.2]** Alternatively, by dragging the white point towards the middle, the lightest areas of the image are being re-assigned. For instance, if the white point is relocated to level 143, everywhere in the image from level 143 to level 255 is considered pure white. **[FIG. 22.3]** Moving

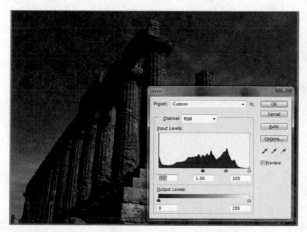

FIGURE 22.2 Sliding the Black Point towards the center darkens the image by remapping all levels below the Black Point to black.

FIGURE 22.3 Sliding the White Point towards the center lightens the image by remapping all levels above the White Point to white.

gamma to the left or right will reassign the mid-point—sliding towards the black point will make a lighter image and towards the white point will make a darker image. Moving the gray point towards the white point reassigns the luminosity values for areas in the image that are between 50% gray and black; it makes more of the luminosity information within the image favor the darker side. Small adjustments to the black-point and the white-point sliders towards the middle in the input levels are a fast and effective way to give your image a greater range. **[FIG. 22.4]**

The **output level** information on the bottom allows reassignment of luminosity information by limiting the darks or lights in the image. Moving the black point slider towards the right will effectively eliminate shadow information below that point, making a grayer image. **[FIG. 22.5]** Dragging the white point towards the left will eliminate highlight information. The black point and the white point in the output levels may be reversed.

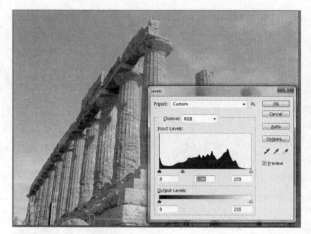

FIGURE 22.4 Adjusting Gamma towards the left lighten the image.

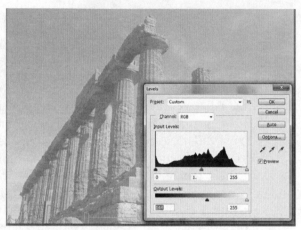

FIGURE 22.5 Adjusting the Black Output level clips all levels below the Black Point to gray.

The **Curves** tool **[FIG. 22.6]** provides refined adjustment of the luminosity values of an image. The Curves tool is based on a grid that shows the relationship between the original values of the image (input) and the adjustment (output). The input values are represented by the horizontal axis and the output by the vertical axis with the histogram appearing along the bottom. The diagonal line running through the grid is the default curve that is used to refine tonal adjustments.

By placing points on the curve and bending the curve up or down, input values are reassigned to their correlating locations on the output scale. For instance, placing a point in the middle of the line and bending the curve upwards creates a lighter image because level 128 is now reassigned to a lighter (higher number) value. **[FIG. 22.7]** Many points can be placed on the curve to make very subtle adjustments, but usually no more than five are needed to get an optimal tonal range; two or three can

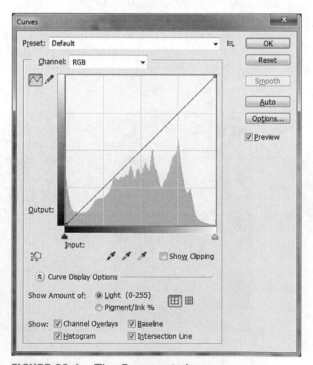

FIGURE 22.6 The Curves window

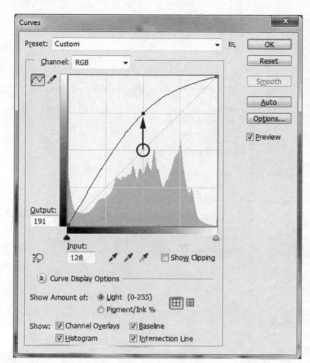

FIGURE 22.7   The Curve adjusted to make an image lighter by remapping 50% gray (level 128) to level 191.

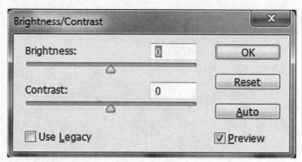

FIGURE 22.8   Brightness and Contrast Adjustment

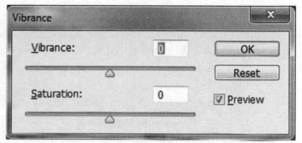

FIGURE 22.9   Vibrance adjustment

typically perform the needed adjustment. To remove a point on the curve, drag the point off the curves window. As with the Levels tool, these adjustments can be made in the composite channel or the component color channels.

Brightness/Contrast [FIG. 22.8] quickly adjusts the brightness (amount of white or black) as well as the contrast (concentrations of tones on either side of the luminosity scale).

Vibrance [FIG. 22.9] adjusts color intensity in the image. Saturation will make all colors intensify in the image, whereas vibrance will only intensify non-skin-tone (cooler) colors.

Use **Hue/Saturation [FIG. 22.10]** to change colors throughout an image or selection.

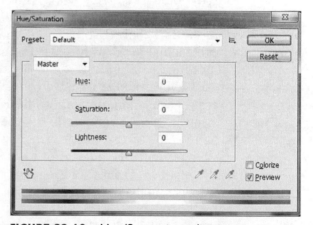

FIGURE 22.10   Hue/Saturation adjustment

Hue/Saturation provides adjustments for hue (meaning the color), saturation (color intensity), and brightness (the amount of white or black mixed in with the color). This Hue/Saturation window shows two color ramps at the bottom to compare the original input color with the changes (output). If colorize is selected, the image will turn into a monotone image (meaning a single color and white make up the image information). Discrete hue areas may be adjusted as well without affecting other areas by clicking the dropdown menu above the adjustments.

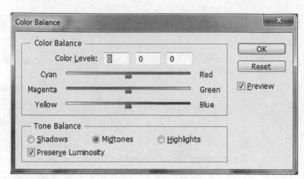

FIGURE 22.11 Color Balance adjustment

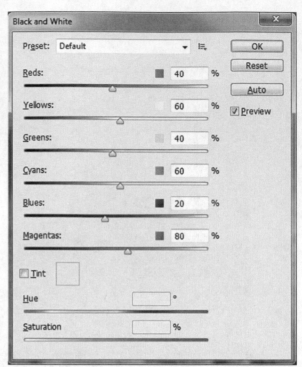

FIGURE 22.12 Black and White adjustment

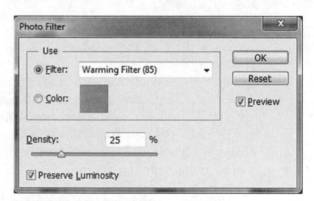

FIGURE 22.13 Photo Filter adjustment

Color balance [FIG. 22.11] provides adjustments based on Cyan–Red, Magenta–Green, and Yellow–Blue tones in the image. These adjustments can take place in either the shadows, midtones, or highlight areas of the image.

Black and White [FIG. 22.12] turns color images into black and white by providing fine-tuning controls for general color areas (Reds, Yellows, Greens, Cynas, Blues, and Magentas). A colorization option is provided with the tint control at the bottom of the window.

Photo Filter [FIG. 22.13] overlays color overtop the image in order to change an image's temperature (warm, cool). Use the drop down for many presets and the density slider for more or less of an effect.

Invert will make the negative of the image by inverting each luminosity level within component channels (i.e., level 1 will become level 255).

Posterize limits the amount of tonal values in each component channel of the image; lower values produce high contrast images with fewer colors.

Threshold [FIG. 22.14] creates a high contrast version of an image or selection by either assigning black or white to each pixel based on luminosity values. Any value between the left-hand side of the histogram (black) and the threshold point will be reassigned to black. Anything to the right will be reassigned to white.

Gradient Map will take a predefined gradient and replace the colors in a photograph while retaining the luminosity values.

Desaturate removes all color information and creates a black and white image.

FIGURE 22.14 Threshold adjustment

Replace color [FIG. 22.15] provides the ability to change a selected color to a different color by using hue, saturation, and/or brightness. Replace color works very much the same as color range whereas a selection is based on a color sample and a fuzziness setting.

All of these adjustments appear as **adjustment layers** in the layers panel providing for non-destructive editing (see Chapter 18).

FIGURE 22.15   Replace Color adjustment

CHAPTER 23

Color

The default file type for Photoshop is **RGB** (Red, Green, and Blue). This is a color space used specifically for images that will appear on any hardware that projects light to produce an image: a monitor, projector, or smart phone, for instance. The three component channels represent the strength of that particular color as a luminosity level from 0 (black) to 255 (white). For example, if there is pure white in the Red channel, the color represented in the composite (RGB) channel will be pure red. The **CMYK** (cyan, magenta, yellow, and black) mode is used for any image that will eventually be produced on some kind of surface (i.e., magazines, posters, or postcards). Each channel in CMYK represents an amount of ink (between 0 and 100%) that will be placed on a surface. **Grayscale** mode has no color information but retains 256 levels of tonal information. **Bitmap** is a color mode where there is only black; pixels are either turned on or off. **Indexed color** is a mode that uses a color palette that is limited to 256 colors only. **LAB** color is the intermediate color model Photoshop uses when converting from one color mode to another. LAB has a lightness component (L) that can range from 0 to 100. The *a* component (green–red axis) and the *b* component (blue–yellow axis) can range from +127 to –128.

Use IMAGE menu > MODE to change from one color model to another. With any of these conversions, changes will take place to the visible color in the file. Converting from RGB to CMYK will shift colors because CMYK color has a smaller overall amount of colors than RGB; there will be a detectable shift in blues. To get into Bitmap mode the image must be switched to Grayscale first and then to Bitmap.

The Color Picker window can be accessed by double clicking the foreground or background color icon on the toolbar or the color panel. [FIG. 23.1] The Color Picker window provides various models for selecting and modifying color, including RGB, CMYK, HSB (Hue, Saturation, Brightness), LAB, Web Safe colors, as well as Color Libraries. In the **HSB** model, **hue** refers to a place along the color wheel (i.e., Red, Orange, Yellow, Green, Blue, Indigo, Violet and back to red again) and is represented by a degree between 0 and 360. **Saturation** is the intensity of the color—from gray to full intensity—and is represented by a scale from 0 to 100%. **Brightness** refers to how much black or white is mixed with color and is also represented by a scale from 0 to 100%. Within the Color Picker window, the spectrum ramp in the center of the window refers to hue and within the large square the horizontal range refers to saturation and the vertical range refers to brightness. Selecting the S or the B in the HSB color selection area will rearrange the range of the square and the ramp. For S the ramp will represent saturation, for B it will represent brightness.

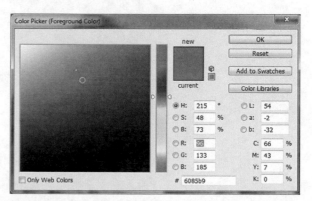

FIGURE 23.1   The Color Picker window

CHAPTER 24

Gradients

The Gradient tool creates a precise transition of color and/or transparency. **[FIG. 24.1]** Gradients can be used to fill the entire canvas or fill within a selection. Drawing a gradient involves select-

FIGURE 24.1   Gradient options

ing a **predefined gradient** from the gradient palette on the option bar, selecting the type of gradient (linear, radial, angular, reflected gradient, or diamond gradient), and then drawing a line inside the canvas to define the beginning and end of the gradient. The beginning and end points can be anywhere inside or outside the canvas.

To create or edit a gradient, click on the thumbnail preview in the options panel; the gradient editor will appear. **[FIG. 24.2]** The gradient editor lists the predefined gradients at the top of the window; any of these can be selected to use as the basis for editing. At the bottom of the gradient editor is a preview of the selected gradient. The **opacity** stops on top, refer to the opacity at that particular location of the gradient. When an opacity stop is selected, the opacity option will be activated (a number between 0 and 100% can be selected) as will the location option, which is the place along the gradient path where the transparency occurs. New opacity stops can be added by clicking on the top of the path and can be removed by clicking and dragging them up and away from the preview. There will also be the option to change the **point of transition** (a small diamond); this can be placed anywhere between 5 and 95% between the opacity stops. Below the preview is where **color stops** are selected. The

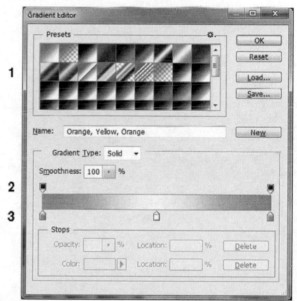

FIGURE 24.2   The Gradient Editor—1. Gradient Presets 2. Opacity Stops 3.Color Stops

color can be changed by clicking on the stop itself or clicking on the color selector at the bottom of the editor. The color stop can also be set to be the **current foreground** or **background color** by selecting that option in color option. Location of the stops can be controlled the same way as transparency—by sliding them along the path or typing in a location number. Color stops can be added and subtracted the same way as well as by changing the transition point. Save a custom gradient by typing in a name and clicking New.

CHAPTER 25

Image Size/Crop/Canvas Size

The Image Size tool (IMAGE menu > IMAGE SIZE) is used to change the physical size and resolution of images. Image size displays the number of pixels (horizontally and vertically) that make up the size of the image. The total number of pixels is displayed at the top of the window. **[FIG. 25.1]** The **document size** reflects the overall size of the physical file by dividing the number of pixels by the resolution (in inches). The size can be displayed as a percentage (100% is the full image width) or in centimeters, millimeters, points, picas, or columns. Changes to the size of the image can be controlled two ways: 1.) change the document size and 2.) change the overall pixel dimensions. Increasing the size of the image will add pixels to the image; decreasing the size of your image will remove pixels from

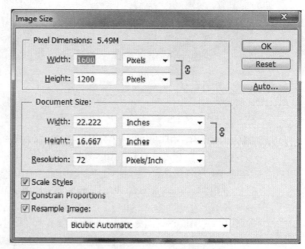

FIGURE 25.1   Image Size window

the image. The resolution will remain the same. Changing the **pixel dimensions** either uses pixels or a percentage to control the size. By typing in either a number of pixels or a percentage, the overall size of the image changes and is reflected in the document size settings.

The **resolution** can be changed in Image Size as well. For print purposes, files typically need to be 300 pixels per inch (PPI) or larger; for web purposes, a resolution of 72 PPI will suffice. NOTE: Increasing the resolution in a lower-resolution image (an image pulled off the web for instance) will not make the image any clearer. Photoshop is **interpolating** this information by making a best guess as to what pixels *should* exist between existing pixels. Photoshop does not know what the world looks like outside of the image. Changing the amount of pixels in the image—either increasing or decreasing—is referred to as **resampling.** Photoshop provides five methods of resampling based on the type of image or whether the file will be resized or scaled down. To change the resolution without adding or subtracting information, uncheck the **resample image** box; the overall image size will get larger or smaller based on the new number. Image size can be changed unequally in two directions by unchecking the **constrain proportions** box.

The Crop tool **[FIG. 25.2]** is used to resize an image by decreasing (or increasing) the canvas size. When the Crop tool is selected, it will place a frame over the entire image, drag the corners to change the size of the canvas. **[FIG. 25.3]** If a specific proportion is desired, use one of the ratios in the

FIGURE 25.2   Crop tool

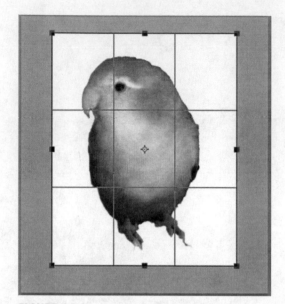

FIGURE 25.3 Active Crop window

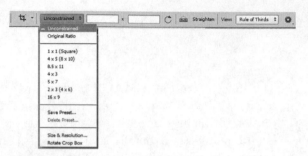

FIGURE 25.4 Crop Proportion presets

dropdown menu on the options bar or type in custom dimensions for width and height. **[FIG. 25.4]** Different grids can be superimposed over the image in order to specify interest areas. The crop frame may be rotated as well to account for images that need some straightening.

The Canvas Size tool (IMAGE menu > CANVAS SIZE) is used to add space or decrease the working space (canvas) of an image. **[FIG. 25.5]** It will not increase or decrease the size of the actual image. **Units** of measurement can be in inches, pixels, percentages, metric, or typographical units. Choose where the image will be **anchored** by selecting one of the nine boxes in the grid on Canvas Size window—Bottom left or right, Top left or right, Left, right, top, bottom, or middle are the options. Increasing the size of the canvas will add the background color to the new areas. **Canvas extension color** refers to the color of added pixels—this can be defined as background, foreground, white, black, 50% gray, or a selected color. Decreasing the size of the canvas will show the prompt "the new canvas size is smaller than the current canvas size" with an option to proceed or cancel.

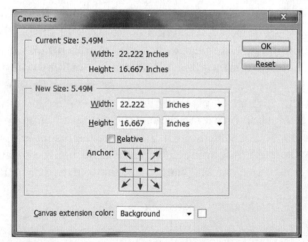

FIGURE 25.5 Canvas Size window

CHAPTER 26

Type in Photoshop

Type can be placed into a file by selecting the Type tool **[FIG. 26.1]** and clicking on the screen or creating a rectangular shape to define an area for the text. **[FIG. 26.2]** Type can be placed horizontally or vertically. **[FIG. 26.2]** A type layer is created for each instance of type; the name of the layer will reflect the characters typed. **[FIG. 26.4]** All adjustments layers, layer masks, as well as layer effects can be used with type. To select type, use the Type tool to make a selection of individual characters or the whole phrase or double click the type layer to select all of the characters in the type layer.

FIGURE 26.1   Type tool

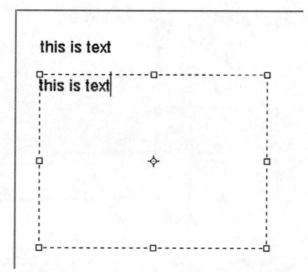

FIGURE 26.2   Two ways to place type in Photoshop. Click on the screen and begin typing (above), or define a rectangular window and type inside (below)

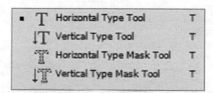

FIGURE 26.3   Type tools

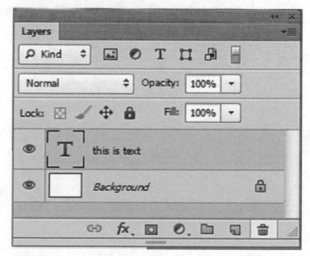

FIGURE 26.4   A Type layer

The Character panel [FIG. 25.5] shares many of the same controls as Illustrator and InDesign. Additional controls provides the ability to make a **faux bold** for typefaces without a bold style and a **faux italic** for typefaces without an italic style. The method of rendering type—the **anti-aliasing method**—can be changed to one of five different settings: none, sharp, crisp, strong, and smooth. Type layers may also be warped. With the Type tool and a type layer selected, click the Warped type icon on the options panel. The tool will provide a list of predefined warps to reshape the type; the warps can be customized with a bend percentage in the horizontal and vertical direction. [FIG. 25.6] Type may still be edited if it has been warped.

To make type as a selection, use the Type mask tool (associated with the Type tool.) Using this tool will create a selection from typed characters. After the type mask is created, it will not be editable anymore as type.

FIGURE 26.5 The Character panel

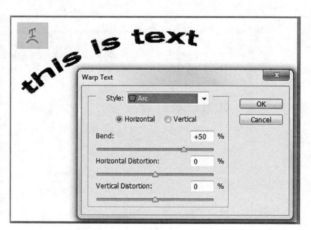

FIGURE 26.6 Warped text

CHAPTER 27

Blending Modes

The blending mode specified in the options panel or in the layers panel [**FIG. 27.1**] controls how pixels in the image are affected by an editing tool or by layering in an image. It's helpful to keep the following terms in mind when visualizing a blending mode's effect. The base color is the original color in the image or the bottom-most layer. The blend color is the color being applied with the Painting or Editing tool or as a new layer. The result color is the color resulting from the blend.

The **Normal** mode is the default mode and creates fully opaque pixels; blending can only occur by changing the transparency. The **Dissolve** mode creates fully opaque pixels but in the style of a bitmap image where pixels are either turned on or off—there are no smooth-color transitions. As the dissolve layer becomes more transparent, the pixels will break up in a random manner. The **Behind** mode (only seen in the fill command or editing tools) places pixels on the transparent part of a layer.

The next group of blending modes uses the darker side of the luminosity scale to have an effect—pure white will have no effect in these modes. The **Darken** mode looks at the color information in each channel and selects the darker base or blend components to make the resulting color. Pixels that are lighter than the blend color will be replaced and tinted with the blend color; pixels darker than the blend color will not change. The **Multiply** mode looks at the color information in each channel and multiplies the base color by the blend color. Multiply, in this instance, means that white is considered 1 and black is considered 0; multiplying by 1 (white) will have no effect, however, multiplying by anything less than 1 will result in a darker color.

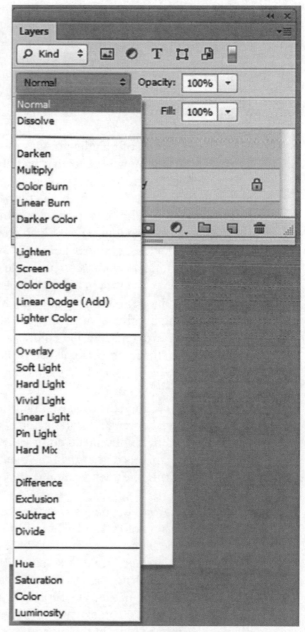

FIGURE 27.1 Blending Modes in the Layers panel

73

Multiplying any color with black (0) produces black. The **Color Burn** mode looks at the color information in each channel and darkens the base color with the darkest components of the blend color to increase the contrast. Blending with white produces no change. The **Linear Burn** mode looks at the color information in each channel and darkens the base color with the darkest components of the blend color by decreasing the brightness (adding black). Blending with white produces no change. The **Darker Color** mode selects the darkest color in either the base or blend color as the result color; there is no mixing of component information in this mode.

The next group of blending modes uses the lighter side of the luminosity scale to have an effect— pure black will have no effect in these modes. The **Lighten** mode looks at the color information in each channel and selects the brighter base or blend components to make the resulting color. The **Screen** mode looks at the color information in each channel and multiplies the inverse of the base color and the blend color. In this instance, inverse means that white is considered 0 and black is considered 1. Multiplying by 1 (black) will have no effect; however, multiplying by anything less than 1 will result in a darker color. Multiplying any color with white (0) produces white. The **Color Dodge** mode looks at the color information in each channel and brightens the base color with the brightest components of the blend color to decrease the contrast. The **Linear Dodge** mode looks at the color information in each channel and brightens the base color with the brightest components of the blend color by increasing the brightness (adding white). The **Lighter Color** mode selects the brightest color in either the base or blend color as the result color; there is no mixing of component information in this mode.

The next group of blending modes uses both the darkest and lightest information of the luminosity scale—50% gray will have no effect in these modes. The **Overlay** mode multiplies or screens the colors, depending on the base color. Blend color overlays the existing pixels while preserving the highlights and shadows of the base color. The base color is not replaced but is mixed with the blend color to reflect the lightness or darkness of the original color. The **Soft Light** mode darkens or lightens the colors, depending on the blend color. Painting with pure black or white produces a distinctly darker or lighter area but does not result in pure black or white. The **Hard Light** mode multiplies or screens the colors, depending on the blend color. If the blend color is lighter than 50% gray, the image is lightened, as in the screen mode. If the blend color is darker than 50% gray, the image is darkened, as in multiply mode. Painting with pure black or white results in pure black or white. This mode is used for adding highlights or shadows to an image. The **Vivid Light** mode burns or dodges the colors by increasing or decreasing the contrast, depending on the blend color. If the blend color is lighter than 50% gray, the image is lightened by decreasing the contrast. If the blend color is darker than 50% gray, the image is darkened by increasing the contrast. The **Linear Light** mode burns or dodges the colors by decreasing or increasing the brightness, depending on the blend color. If the blend color is lighter than 50% gray, the image is lightened by increasing the brightness. If the blend color is darker than 50% gray, the image is darkened by decreasing the brightness. The **Pin Light** mode replaces the colors, depending on the blend color as in the darker/lighter color mode. If the blend color is lighter than 50% gray, pixels darker than the blend color are replaced, and pixels lighter than the blend color do not change. If the blend color is darker than 50% gray, pixels lighter than the blend color are replaced.

The next group of modes performs calculations on the component channel luminosity levels to achieve the result color. The **Difference** mode looks at the color information in each channel and subtracts either the blend color from the base color or the base color from the blend color, depending on which has the greater brightness value. Blending with white inverts the base color values; blending with black produces no change. The **Exclusion** mode creates an effect similar to but lower in contrast than the Difference mode. The **Subtract** mode subtracts the information in the blend layer channels from the base layer channels; any negative number is clipped to zero (pure black). The **Divide** mode divides the information in the blend layer channels from the base layer channels; any result greater than one is clipped to one (pure white).

The remaining blending modes affect hue, saturation, and luminosity information. The **Hue** mode creates a result color with the luminance and saturation of the base color and the hue of the blend color. The **Saturation** mode creates a result color with the luminance and hue of the base color and the saturation of the blend color. Painting with this mode in an area with no (0) saturation (gray) causes no change. The **Color** mode creates a result color with the luminance of the base color and the hue and saturation of the blend color. This preserves the tonal information in the image and is useful for coloring monochrome images or for tinting color images. The **Luminosity** mode creates a result color with the hue and saturation of the base color and the luminance of the blend color.

CHAPTER 28

Image Retouching

Tools for retouching images include the **Clone Stamp, Spot Healing brush, Healing brush, Patch tool, Content Aware Move,** and **Content Aware Fill.** All of these tools utilize sampled areas of the image to paint in or replace areas that are

FIGURE 28.1 The Clone Stamp tool

unwanted. The **Clone Stamp [FIG. 28.1]** uses all available paint brushes and blending modes to sample an area and paint over another area. To use the tool, find an area to sample, hold down the Alt/Opt key and click to mark that as the location of sampled pixels. Proceed by stamping in sampled pixels into an area that needs to be touched up. In the options bar, align refers to keeping the sampled area constantly aligned with the painting area. **[FIG. 28.2]** Unchecking will sample from the same location

for each brush stroke. **Sample** refers to whether the sample is taken from current layers, current & below layers, or all layers. The Clone Stamp typically works best if the brush has a softer edge and if the sampled area is periodically moved to avoid unwanted patterning.

FIGURE 28.2 Clone Stamp options

The **Spot Healing brush [FIG. 28.3]** is used to quickly remove blemishes by sampling from areas around the spot and painting in with them. The Spot Healing brush uses basic brush settings (size, hardness, spacing, and angle) and can use a limited range of blending modes.

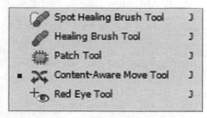

FIGURE 28.3 Retouching tools

The **Healing brush** (associated with the Spot Healing brush) is similar to the Spot Healing brush but is typically used over larger areas. The Healing brush uses samples from areas surrounding the area to be retouched and also matches the texture, lighting and transparency of the sampled areas. The Healing brush uses basic brush settings (size, hardness, spacing and angle) and can use a limited range of blending modes.

The **Patch tool** (associated with the Spot Healing Brush) uses a selection based approach to retouching areas. The Patch tool works two ways, either by selecting the area to be retouched (source) or by selecting a sampled area (destination.) To use the **source** method, create a lasso selection with the Patch tool of the area to be retouched and then drag and release the selection over an area to be used as the sample. **[FIG. 28.4]** To use the **destination** method create a lasso selection over the sampled area and then drag and release over the area to be retouched. **[FIG. 28.5]**

The **Content Aware Move** (associated with the Spot Healing brush) tool provides the ability to create a selection around a part of an image that needs to be moved (a person in a field for instance), move just that part of the image, and have Photoshop fill in the selected area. To use Content Aware Move, draw a selection around part of the image and drag it to a new location. Photoshop will analyze the image in order to create a texture to fill in where the image used to be and also merge the selection

FIGURE 28.4 The Patch tool in Source Mode— 1. Select the source to be retouched. 2. Drag to an area with pixels to fill in the selection. 3. The source is filled and matched with pixels based on the dragged to area.

FIGURE 28.5 The Patch tool in Destination Mode—1. Select the Fill area. 2. Drag the selection to the unwanted area. 3. The dragged to area is filled and matched with selected pixels.

with its new location. After the move occurs, the adaptation setting can be used to change how strict or loose the analysis is in generating new image information. **[FIG. 28.6]**

Content Aware Fill is located in the EDIT > FILL tool and is used to fill in a selected area with information surrounding the selection.

Note: The results of the Healing brush, Patch tool, Content Aware Move, and Content Aware Fill will most likely never be perfect and will always require some touch-ups using the Clone Stamp to clean up the retouching. Always copy the background layer when doing touch-ups so that the original image is not destroyed.

FIGURE 28.6 The Content Aware Match tool— 1. Select the area to Move. 2. Drag to new location. 3. Photoshop blends moved selection with new area.

CHAPTER 29

Filters

There are a tremendous number of effects that can be used in Photoshop within the Filters menu. This section will not cover all of them, but instead will provide a framework for understanding how the filters work. Frequently used filters, however, will be addressed.

The FILTER menu > FILTER GALLERY [FIG. 29.1] houses a large selection of filters that may be used on an entire image or a selection. All of the Filters have various settings based on the particular effect to be achieved. Filters that employ a texture can use the default list of textures or may use any Photoshop file by selecting it from the Context menu next to the Texture list. [FIG. 29.2] Multiple filters may be used at the same time by clicking the **new effect layer** from

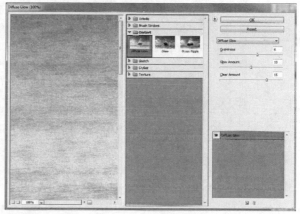

FIGURE 29.1 The Filter Gallery Preview area (left), Available Filters (middle), and Filter Controls and Filter Layering (right)

the Filter Gallery window. Filters will be stacked as in the layers panel; the filters at the top of the list will affect the results from the filters below, and the effect layers can be reordered. [FIG. 29.3]

To provide a high degree of flexibility within the workflow, convert layers to Smart Objects by using the FILTER menu > CONVERT FOR SMART FILTERS. When filters are applied to Smart Objects they are listed below them in the layers panel. [FIG. 29.4] Filters can later be adjusted by double clicking their name in the layers panel and can be turned on and off and can also have their order rearranged if multiple filters are being used.

FIGURE 29.2 Texture options for some filters; the context menu provides the ability to pick other textures

FIGURE 29.3 Stacking multiple filters

FIGURE 29.4 Smart Object layers with filters applied

79

Under the FILTER menu > BLUR are many ways to blur an image or a selected portion of an image. The most commonly used Blur Filter is **Gaussian Blur, [FIG. 29.5]** which uniformly blurs an image and can use a scale from .1 pixels to 1000 pixels. Other commonly used blurs are **Motion Blur, [FIG. 29.6]** which blurs along a specified angle, and **Radial Blur, [FIG. 29.7]** which blurs around the center.

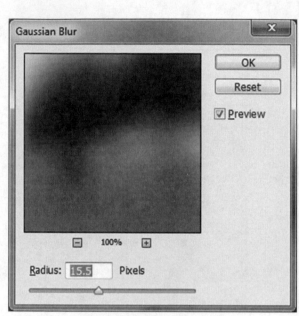

FIGURE 29.5   Gaussian Blur filter

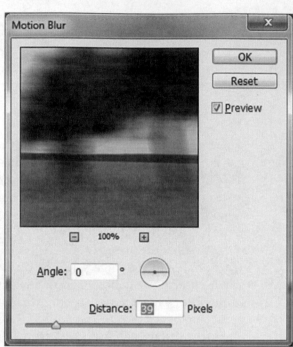

FIGURE 29.6   Motion Blur filter

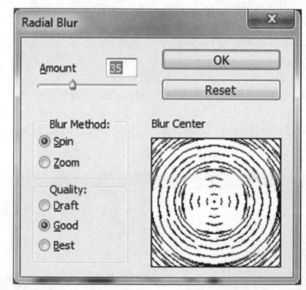

FIGURE 29.7   Radial Blur filter

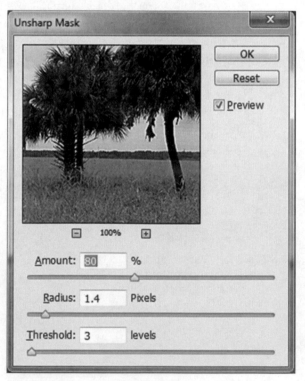

FIGURE 29.8   Unsharp Mask filter

Unsharp Mask, [FIG. 29.8] which is found under the FILTER menu > SHARPEN, is used to make images appear crisper (unfortunately it cannot make an out of focus image in focus). The

Unsharp Mask works by increasing the contrast in areas of the image that have a difference in tonal value; this is an optical illusion that makes the image appear crisper. There are three parameters in the filter—**Amount, Radius,** and **Threshold. Amount** is the strength of the application of the filter. **Radius** refers to how many pixels on either side of an area of contrast will be affected. **Threshold** refers to how different neighboring tonal values have to be in order for the effect to take place. A higher threshold setting will make for a lower effect on the image. There are no "standard" settings for the Unsharp Mask—the values will vary greatly depending on the type of image. An image with a lot of texture will vary from one with open, smooth areas. Typically, set the amount to the highest value possible so that the image does not look overly adjusted, and then drag the radius up until little halos begin to present themselves (this is an exaggerated sharpening effect). A low threshold setting—between 1 and 5—usually will suffice for most images.

Use the FILTER menu > RENDER filters to either generate randomized areas as the basis for texture effects (**Clouds, Difference Clouds,** and **Fibers**) or to create **Lens Flares** and **Lighting Effects** Clouds **[FIG. 29.9]** will create a texture of clouds using the foreground and background colors. Difference Clouds **[FIG. 29.10]** will have the same effect as Clouds but will apply the filter using the Difference blending mode. Fibers **[FIG. 29.11]** create a texture of fibers by changing the variance and strength. Lighting effects **[FIG. 29.12]** will create the illusion that a light is being shone on the image—different types, strengths, and color lights can be chosen as well as the way the surface reflects light.

FIGURE 29.9   Render Clouds filter

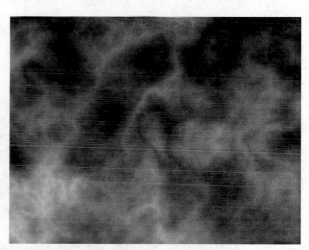

FIGURE 29.10   Difference Clouds filter

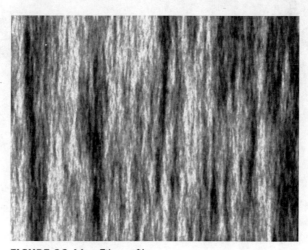

FIGURE 29.11   Fibers filter

Multiple lights can be created and are arranged similar to the Filter Gallery.

Use the FILTER menu > NOISE to either add noise to an image or to reduce it. **Add Noise [FIG. 29.13]** applies a randomized coverage of pixels based on an amount percentage. Choose Mono-chromatic to only have black and white noise. **Dust and Scratches [FIG. 29.14]** is used to reduce overall surface noise in an image based on an amount and threshold setting.

The **Liquify** filter **[FIG. 29.15]** provides the ability to move image information around as if it was liquid. The Liquify filter opens up a new window to perform the effect. The **Forward Warp** tool will push pixels around the surface based on **brush size** and **brush pressure**—the larger the brush, the more image information it will include, and the higher the pressure the stronger the effect will be. Other tools include a reconstruct tool (undoes liquefaction), **Twirl** (spins information around the center of the brush), **Pucker, Bloat,** and **Push Left.** The brush will continue to have an effect so long as the mouse button is held down, even if the cursor is not moving. Use **Restore all** to revert back to the unaltered image.

FIGURE 29.12 Lighting Effects filter

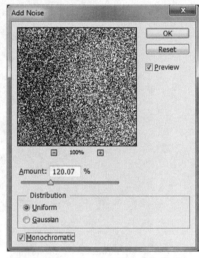

FIGURE 29.13 Add Noise filter

FIGURE 29.14 Dust and Scratches filter

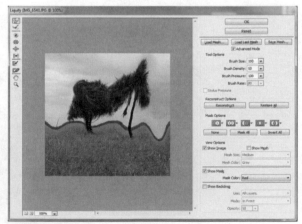

FIGURE 29.15 Liquify filter

CHAPTER 30

File Types

Photoshop can open and save files in a variety of formats. The most common ones are **TIF, JPG,** and **PSD.** A TIF file is an uncompressed image, which will retain all information from the original scan. This is best for files with no layers and limited alpha channel information that need to preserve all the original data. A **JPG** is a file type that compresses the image data to make a smaller file size. JPG only works with files with no layers or alpha channels. JPGs are commonly used for websites, and the image quality will not be the highest because of the compression. Compression can be set from 1 to 12, with 12 being the maximum quality. **[FIG. 30.1] PSD** files refer to Photoshop native format and can save layers, channels, text layers, adjustment layers, etc. This type is best for saving the original composed image. All files can be saved to other formats by using the FILE menu > SAVE AS. Depending on the file type, some file information will be lost; for instance, saving a layered PSD file to JPG will flatten the image.

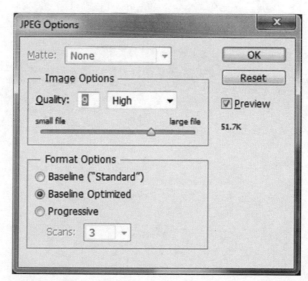

FIGURE 30.1 JPG options

SECTION 3

InDesign

CHAPTER 31

Basics

InDesign is a program used for graphic design layouts and can be used for multi-page documents. The contents of your document are a combination of graphics and text that are typically prepared outside of the program. InDesign works by defining text or graphics frames with shape tools (similar to Illustrator's shaped tools) and then placing content (graphics or text) inside the frames.

The tools on the toolbar **[FIG 31.1]** share similar functions with Illustrator. The **Select** (Move) tool moves items around on screen and can also be use to resize items (use the Shift key to constrain proportions). The **Direct Selection tool** moves content within the frame and can also be used to resize content (use shift key to constrain proportions). The **Pen tool** is used to create custom frames for placing text, graphical content, or solid fills and can be edited the same as objects in Illustrator. Open or closed paths can be filled with content. The **Pencil tool** is used to create freeform shapes for placing text or graphical content. The **Type tool** either creates a rectangular shape to place text within or designates a selected shape as a text frame. The **Frame tools** are used to create frames for content; other options include ellipse and polygon tools. Drawing with these tools will produce shapes with no fill or stroke color. Choosing the tool and then clicking on the screen will bring up a dialog box to define the size of the shape. The **Shape tools** are used to create shapes that have the default fill and stroke colors and work exactly the same as the Frame tool. Graphics or text may be placed inside of these as well. All frames can be edited the same as Illustrator shapes—points can be added or subtracted, points changed to curves, curves edited, etc. The **Line** tool draws straight line segments. The **Transformation** tools include Rotate, Scale, Shear, and Free Transform and are similar to the transformation tools in Illustrator.

FIGURE 31.1 The InDesign toolbar

CHAPTER 32

Creating a New Document

Before starting a new document, consideration must be made as to the page size, the number of pages, the orientation, the number of columns (if applicable), and the margins. All these parameters can be changed during the editing of the file. InDesign uses **points** and **picas** as the default unit of measurement. Points and picas are a traditional typographic unit of measurement whereas 12pts = 1 pica and is written as 1p0. 6 picas (or 6p0) = 1 inch, or 72pts = 1 inch. To change the units of measurement, go to the INDESIGN menu (MAC)/EDIT menu (WIN) >PREFERENCES > UNITS & INCREMENTS to set the desired units: inches, metric, pixels, etc.

[FIG 32.1] InDesign can be used to design a multi-page document; therefore, a **Number of Pages** may be specified in the New Document dialog box. The **Facing Pages** options means that a layout will have a right-hand and left-hand page as in a magazine or book. With facing pages unchecked, each layout will be a singular page. The **Page Size** is specified with a number of built-in defaults for standard page sizes as well as the ability to designate a custom size in the width and height areas. The orientation can be switched from portrait to landscape. **Columns** will divide the page horizontally between the left- and right-hand margins. The term **Gutter** refers to the amount of space between the columns; this can be set as low as 0. The **Margins** for the document are also specified in the dialogue box. If Facing Pages is checked, the margins will have a top, bottom, inside, and outside setting—inside referring to the area next to the binding. If Facing Pages is not checked, the margins will have settings for top, bottom, left, and right. By default, all the measurements are linked together. To set each margin differently, uncheck the chain link icon. All of these settings may be changed throughout the editing of the document.

The page may be divided vertically two ways in InDesign—by using the **baseline grid** or by **creating guides.** The **baseline grid** [FIG 32.2] divides the active area of the layout into evenly spaced rows, and this is typically used to keep

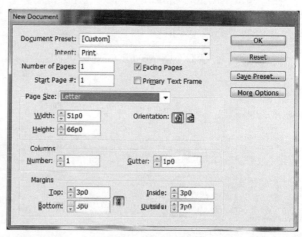

FIGURE 32.1   The New Document window

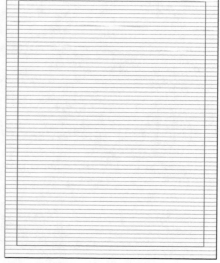

FIGURE 32.2   A new document with default baseline grid of 12pts

type aligned throughout the layout. Turn on the baseline grid by going to the VIEW menu > GRIDS & GUIDES > SHOW BASELINE GRID. Creating guides (LAYOUT menu > CREATE GUIDES) **[FIG 32.3]** will evenly divide the page vertically and horizontally (either between the page edge or margins) into a number of rows or columns; these also use a gutter width **[FIG 32.4]**. Use the Create Guides tool to also get rid of all guides in the layout by selecting **Remove Existing Ruler Guides.**

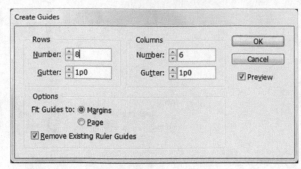

FIGURE 32.3   Create Guides window

The baseline grid can be changed through the INDESIGN menu (MAC)/EDIT menu (WIN) > PREFERENCES > GRIDS. **[FIG 32.5]** The color of the grid lines, start location, and increment of gridlines can be adjusted. To make the grid appear in front of all content, uncheck the **grids in back** button. The grids settings may also be used to create a document grid with evenly spaced horizontal and vertical spaces.

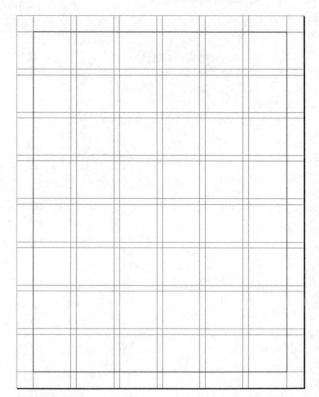

FIGURE 32.4   A document with a matrix of guides (8 rows, 6 columns)

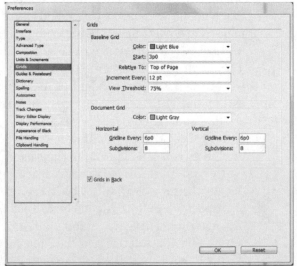

FIGURE 32.5   Grids preferences

The **Pages Panel [FIG 32.6]** is used to navigate through all of the pages in the document. If facing pages was selected when creating the document, the first page (right facing) will appear by itself followed by a spread of a left- and right-hand page. If facing pages was not selected, each page will appear one after another in the panel. Pages can be added using the **Create new page** icon or through **Insert pages** within the page panel context menu. Pages can be deleted by dragging individual or multiple pages to the Trash can icon. To go to a specific page in your layout, double click the page in the pages panel.

To place consistent content, margins, columns, or guides on multiple pages, use the **Master Pages** option at the top of the pages panel. Double click the **A-Master** page thumbnail to create master content. Anything placed or changed within the master page will show on any page that has the **A** symbol on it throughout the document and will not be editable within those pages. To create a new master page, go to the Pages Panel Context menu and select New Master. To apply the new master to pages within the document, either drag the desired master page on top of the specific page thumbnail or go to the Pages Panel Context menu and select **Apply Master.** This will provide options for selecting which master to apply to which pages.

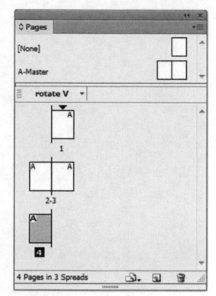

FIGURE 32.6   The Pages panel

CHAPTER 33

Placing Graphical Content

Placing refers to bringing content into InDesign and creates a live link between InDesign and the content. To **place** content, go to the FILE menu > PLACE. **[FIG 33.1]** After selecting the graphic file with the place command, a thumbnail will appear at the end of the cursor. Either click once on the screen to place the image at its full print size, or click and drag the image to resize the image to an appropriate size (these can be resized at a later time). If a content box is selected prior to using the PLACE command, the selected graphic will be placed into that frame or replace any existing graphic within the frame. Use **Import Options** in the Place dialog box to specify layers or specific views of the graphic. The keyboard shortcut for placing is cmd/cntl + D.

Note: **Avoid copying and pasting content into InDesign.** When content is placed, it creates a live link between the graphics and InDesign, which means InDesign will know when changes are made to the original files and will prompt you to update them. If files are copied and pasted, the live link is lost and the content is "frozen in time."

When content is placed, it will appear in the **links panel. [FIG 33.2]** Each entry in the links panel lists the name of the file and its location at the bottom of the panel. InDesign will list all of the information it knows about the file including its name, size, location, and whether it has been changed. The links panel will create alerts when a link has changed or cannot be found and will allow for the link to

FIGURE 33.1 The Place window; use Import Options if specific views of files are preferred

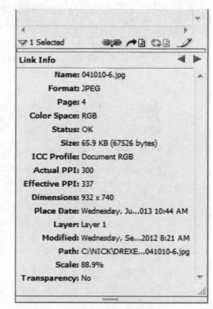

FIGURE 33.2 The Links panel with information showing related to a specific linked file

be updated or replaced with a new link. A **yellow triangle** with an exclamation point next to the name of a link indicates that the original file has changed. Even though the graphic may have been updated outside of InDesign, the original low-res preview will appear in the layout until the link has been updated. Use the **Update link** icon to display the latest version of the graphic. A **red question mark** indicates that the file cannot be found or the file's name and/or location may have changed. **[FIG 33.3]** Use the **Relink** icon to find the current location or to replace it with a new graphic.

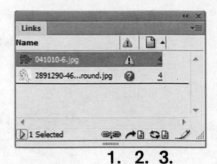

1. 2. 3.

FIGURE 33.3 A link has been changed (triangle with exclamation point); a link is missing (circle with question mark). 1. Relink 2. Go To Link 3. Update Link

The frame and the content are individual components that can be transformed separately. The black arrow moves and resizes the frame, and the white arrow moves and resizes the content. Changing the size of the frame will not change the size of the content. To change the size of both frame and content, use the **black arrow** in conjunction with the **cmd/cntl key;** hold the shift key down to maintain the same proportions.

When a frame is selected with the black arrow, the **measurements** options **[FIG 33.4]** will appear at the top of the InDesign window. The frame's location is displayed as its X and Y coordinates as well as its width and height. The X and Y coordinates are based on the **reference point** specified on the right-hand side of this window. New locations or sizes can be typed into each of the boxes.

FIGURE 33.4 The Measurements bar

Frames may also be transformed by **scaling, rotating, skewing,** or **reflecting.** When content is selected with the white arrow, the measurements will reflect the size and location of the content WITHIN the content frame.

All frames, regardless of whether they hold content or not, can have fills and strokes applied to them in a manner similar to Illustrator. Further stylistic choices include presets for line types including thick and thin combinations, dashes, dots, wavy lines, diamonds, and hash marks. **[FIG 33.5]** InDesign provides a **color panel [FIG 33.6]** to create colors based on the RGB or CMYK models as well as swatch panel to save colors to be used throughout a project.

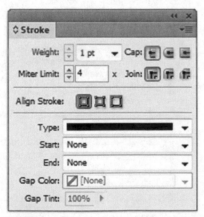

FIGURE 33.5 The Stroke panel

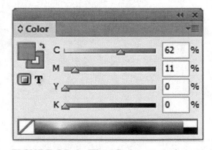

FIGURE 33.6 The Color panel

CHAPTER 34

Fitting, Aligning, and Arranging Content

Besides manually moving and resizing graphical content with the white arrow, content can also be adjusted using the OBJECT menu > FITTING options. **[FIG 34.1] Fill frame proportionally** keeps the graphic in proportion and fills the frame by fitting it to its smaller dimension (either vertical or

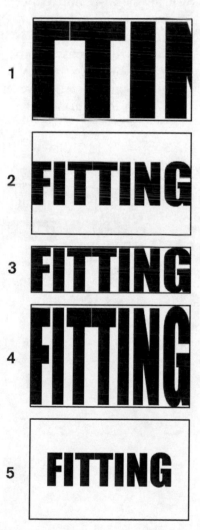

FIGURE 34.1   Fitting options—1. Fill Frame Proportionally 2. Fit Frame Proportionally 3. Fit Frame to Content 4. Fit Content to Frame 5. Center Content

horizontal)—some clipping may occur. **Fit content proportion-ally** keeps the graphic in proportion and fills the frame by fitting it to its larger dimension; this may leave blank space in the content frame. **Fit frame to content** will adjust the size of the frame to accommodate the scaled size of the graphic. **Fit content to frame** will scale the graphic to fit the frame, and the content may be scaled disproportionately. **Center content** will center the scaled graphic within the frame, and proportions will be retained.

FIGURE 34.2   The Align panel

Use the **align panel [FIG 34.2]** to align or distribute objects. Objects can be aligned to their collective left, right, upper, or lower edge as well as their horizontal or vertical centers by using the **Align Objects** options. **[FIG 34.3]** The align panel is found under the WINDOW menu > OBJECT & LAYOUT > ALIGN. A randomly distributed selection of objects can be evenly distributed along their left, right, upper, or lower edge as well as their horizontal or vertical centers by using the **Distribute Objects** options. Select **Use Spacing** to impose a specific amount of space between each object. **[FIG 34.4]** Objects can also be manually aligned to grid, column, or baselines if the VIEW menu > GRIDS & GUIDES > SNAP TO GUIDES is selected.

Use the OBJECT menu >ARRANGE options to move objects above or below other objects. **Bring to front** will move the selected objects to the very top, **bring forward** will move an object higher up in the stacking order, **send backward** will move an object lower in the stacking order, and **send to back** will send an object all the way to the bottom.

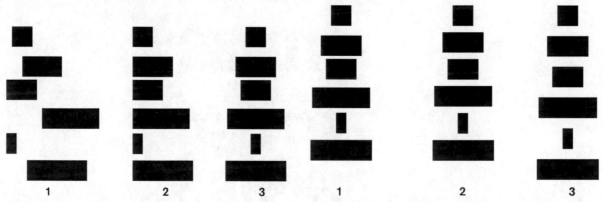

FIGURE 34.3   1. Original Alignment 2. Left Alignment 3. Center Alignment

FIGURE 34.4   1. Original Distribution 2. Distribute Top Edge 3. Distributed using 4p0 spacing

CHAPTER 35

The Character and Paragraph Panel

The **Character Panel [FIG 35.1]** is used to make adjustments to type. The panel is located under the WINDOW menu > TYPE & TABLES > CHARACTER or by using cmd/ctrl + T. The first dropdown menu refers to the **typeface name.** Typefaces with a triangle pointing to the right means that there are different **styles** (bold, italic, etc.) of the typeface, all of which will be listed in the panel below. Otherwise, there will only be a regular version of the typeface available. The **font size** is listed below the style drop-down. **Leading [FIG 35.2]** refers to the space between lines of text, from baseline (bottom of the character) to baseline. By default, leading is the height of the text plus 20% (i.e., 12pts + 2.4pts = 14.4pts). Leading smaller than the default will create lines of text that appear denser and darker; a higher number will create lines that are more open and lighter. **Kerning [FIG 35.3]** refers to the space between pairs of letters. Many typefaces are designed so that specific pairs of letters have the proper amount of spacing (i.e., WA, To, fi, CO, etc.). The kerning adjustment allows the designer to further adjust letter pairs—this may be for typefaces that, when scaled to larger sizes, lose their spacing or typefaces that have not been designed with preset kerning. Use the **Optical** setting to allow InDesign to make a best guess as to proper spacing. The units are 1/1000 of an em space (the width of an upper-case M) and can be set either positive or negative.

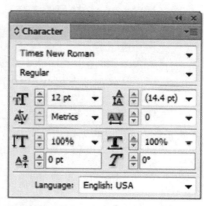

FIGURE 35.1 The Character panel

At harit enti doluptaerum autem is nullab iliquae qui dere corione ssequamus andelluptat eius eatquis aut res delitia simpor sectorum laccus ab iur, eius eos rerorae vento est

At harit enti doluptaerum autem is nullab iliquae qui dere corione ssequamus andelluptat eius eatquis aut res delitia simpor sectorum laccus ab iur, eius eos rerorae vento est

FIGURE 35.2 Auto leading (above); looser leading (below)

FIGURE 35.3 Metrics-based kerning (above); optical-based kerning (below)

Tracking [FIG 35.4] refers to the spacing over the course of a word, sentence, or paragraph. The units are 1/1000 of an em space (the width of an uppercase M) and can be set either positive or negative. **Vertical Scale [FIG 35.5]** will adjust the height of text while maintaining the original width of the letters; text will scale disproportionately. **Horizontal Scale [FIG 35.6]** will adjust the width of text while maintaining the original width of the letters; text will scale disproportionately. Positive or negative percentages may be used for both. **Baseline shift [FIG 35.7]** will shift the text either above or below the originating baseline for the text. **Skew [FIG 35.8]** will create a faux italic in either a positive (forward) or negative (backwards) direction. The character panel's **context menu** provides some further options for text. These include all caps, small caps, superscript, subscript, underline, and strikethrough.

FIGURE 35.4   Unadjusted tracking (above); tracking set to 100 (middle); tracking set to −100 (below)

FIGURE 35.5   Vertical scale at 200%

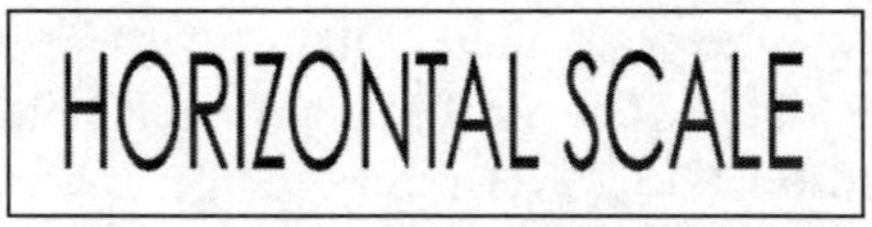

FIGURE 35.6   Horizontal scale at 50%

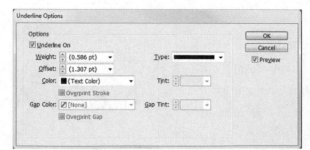

FIGURE 35.7   Baseline shift adjusted above and below baseline

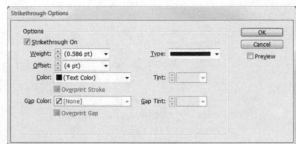

FIGURE 35.8   Skew at 30°

The **underline [FIG 35.9]** and **strikethrough [FIG 35.10]** options in the context menu provide further modifications to these settings. These include a **weight** for the underline; an **offset** (distance) from the baseline; the **color** of the line; and a **style** for the line, tints, and gap colors (colors between dashes). The underline will always be behind the text, and the strikethrough will always appear on top of text.

FIGURE 35.9   Underline options

FIGURE 35.10   Strikethrough options

The **Paragraph panel [FIG 35.11]** is used to make adjustments to entire paragraphs and is located under the WINDOW menu TYPE & TABLES > PARAGRAPH. **Alignment [FIG 35.12]** sets the paragraph so that their left, right, or centers are aligned. **Justification [FIG 35.13]** sets the paragraph with lines of equal length with options that make the last line align to the left, right, center, or are the full

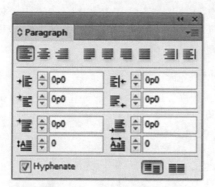

FIGURE 35.11   Paragraph panel

At harit enti doluptaerum autem is nullab iliquae qui dere corione ssequamus andelluptat eius eatquis aut res delitia simpor sectorum laccus ab iur, eius eos rerorae vento est **1**	At harit enti doluptaerum autem is nullab iliquae qui dere corione ssequamus andelluptat eius eatquis aut res delitia simpor sectorum laccus ab iur, eius eos rerorae vento est **2**	At harit enti doluptaerum autem is nullab iliquae qui dere corione ssequamus andelluptat eius eatquis aut res delitia simpor sectorum laccus ab iur, eius eos rerorae vento est **3**

FIGURE 35.12   1. Align Left   2. Align Center   3. Align Right

At harit enti doluptaerum autem is nullab iliquae qui dere corione ssequamus an-delluptat eius eatquis aut res delitia simpor sectorum lac-cus ab iur, eius eos rerorae vento est **1**	At harit enti doluptaerum autem is nullab iliquae qui dere corione ssequamus an-delluptat eius eatquis aut res delitia simpor sectorum lac-cus ab iur, eius eos rerorae vento est **2** At harit enti doluptaerum autem is nullab iliquae qui dere corione ssequamus andell-luptat eius eatquis aut res deli-tia simpor sectorum laccus ab iur, eius eos rerorae vento est **4**	At harit enti doluptaerum autem is nullab iliquae qui dere corione ssequamus an-delluptat eius eatquis aut res delitia simpor sectorum lac-cus ab iur, eius eos rerorae vento est **3**

FIGURE 35.13   1. Justified with last line aligned left   2. Justified with last line centered   3. Justified with last line aligned right   4. All lines justified

width. **Indents Left** and **Right** [FIG 35.14] create a margin for lines of text separate from the inset as defined in text frame options. **First line indent** and **last line indent** [FIG 35.15] will only affect the first or last line of text. **Space before** and **space after** will add space between paragraphs (any block of text where the Return key is used afterwards). **Drop cap** [FIG 35.16] will make a large first (or multiple) character(s) appear on a designated number of lines. The **number of characters** can be defined in the adjacent box. To stop lines of text being hyphenated, uncheck the **hyphenate** box for selected paragraphs. Use **align to baseline grid** [FIG 35.17] to align text to the document's baseline grid independent of the defined leading.

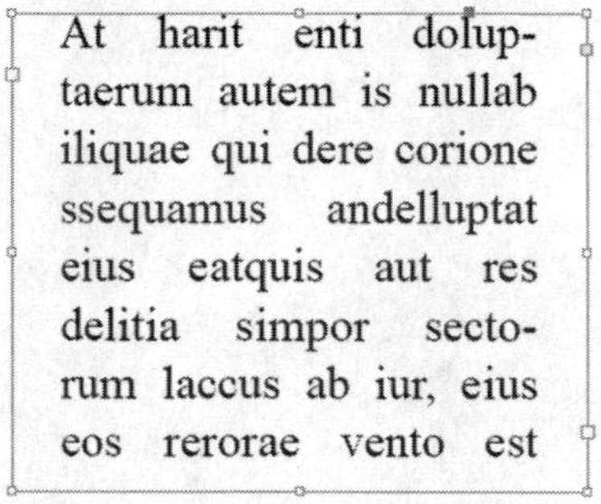

FIGURE 35.14   Left and right indents

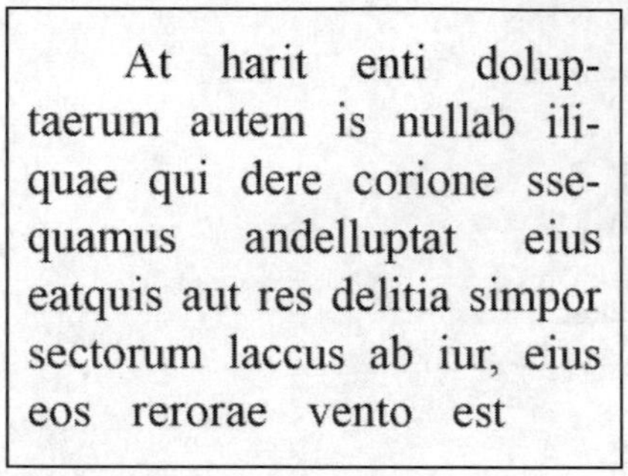

FIGURE 35.15   First and last lines indented

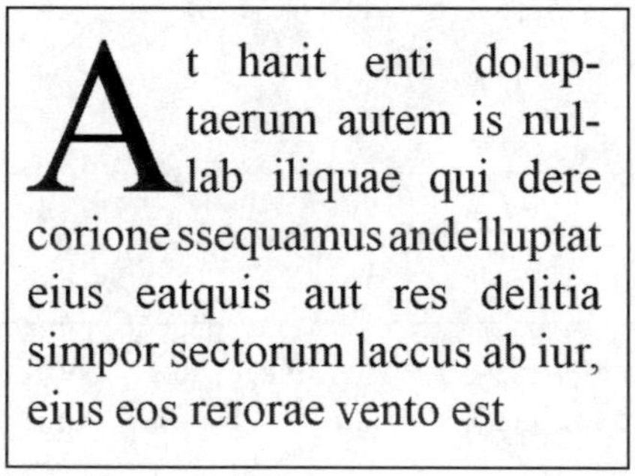

FIGURE 35.16   Three-line drop cap

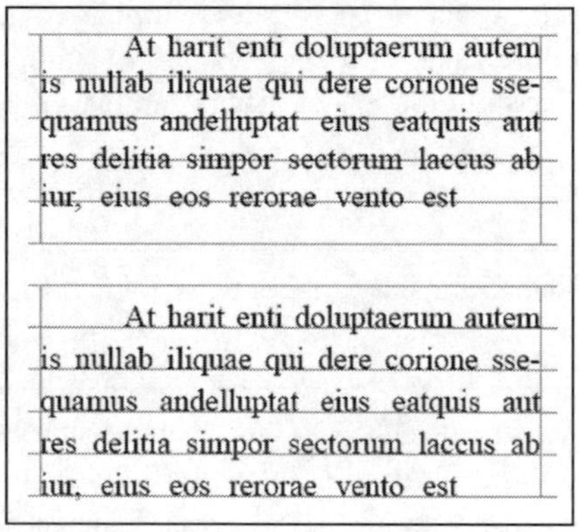

FIGURE 35.17   Text not aligned to baseline grid (above); Aligned with baseline grid (below)

CHAPTER 36

Text Frame Options

Modifications can be adjusted for any frame that holds text using the OBJECT menu > TEXT FRAME OPTIONS (ctrl/cmd + B). **[FIG 36.1]** Text frames may have specific columns of text defined by number and gutter width; the overall width of columns can also be specified. Inset spacing will create an interior margin for the text frame (top, bottom, left, and right). These can be set the same (with the chain link icon) or can be set independently. **[FIG 36.2]** Vertical justification will align text to the top, bottom, center, or justify (all lines of text to fit the text frame). **Ignore text wrap** will ignore objects that are specified to have text wrap around their shape. Under baseline options, **[FIG 36.3]** a **custom baseline grid** can be defined for just the selected text box. The starting location of the grid and the increment of the grid can be defined as well as the color of the gridlines.

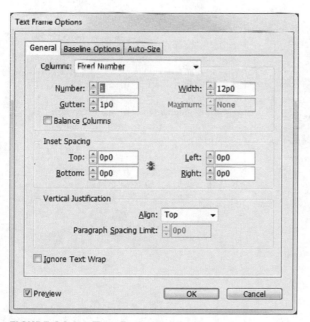

FIGURE 36.1 Text Frame options

At harit enti do-
luptaerum autem is
nullab iliquae qui
dere corione sse-
quamus andelluptat
elus eatquis aut ruo
delitia simpor sec-
torum laccus ab
iur, eius eos rerorae
vento est Oventra-
crum senatudervis
estem et curs in sa
te movirit incem fi-
cepsentriu consus,
orevicae consul hi-

nat. At ad clessum
ocula Satum mur,
nonstrem postrit;
non pul tem, Catu
quit; nuni in re ia
nunum ad auce-
rumus cum maei
publissimo consupi
mplibus? il tem op-
temur estiam der-
cere autem et; no.
Gulius praelis. Opi-
conl oculius, pra re
foraequam non sus
eo vit atuis, quidees

FIGURE 36.2 Two columns created and inset spacing (left and right) applied

FIGURE 36.3 Baseline options in the text frame options window

If there is more text than will fit into a text box, it is referred to as **overset [FIG 36.4]** and will be designated with a red square with a plus sign inside (out port). To accommodate overset text, either edit the text, make the text frame larger, or flow the text into another frame. To flow text from an overset frame to a new frame, click on the out port with the black arrow and either click and drag to define a new text frame or click within an existing empty content frame. **[FIG 36.5]**

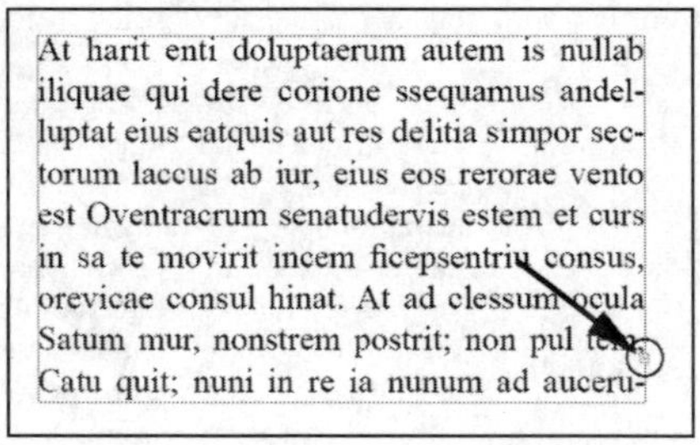

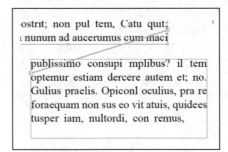

FIGURE 36.4 Overset text and with "out port" showing

FIGURE 36.5 Threaded text

CHAPTER 37

More Typography

As seen with the character panel, there are many considerations to be made with the placement of type. Following are some more tools in InDesign used to consider type as a design element in layouts.

When a layout needs a text element and the copy is not finished, use the TYPE menu > FILL WITH PLACEHOLDER TEXT to fill text frames with some stand-in text. Because the text placed is broken into words (derived from Latin) it gives the appearance of actual copy.

Special characters such as **symbols, markers, hyphens & dashes,** and **quotation marks** are located under the TYPE menu > INSERT SPECIAL CHARACTER. Within the SYMBOLS submenu, there are shortcuts to place bullets (•), copyright symbols (©), ellipsis (…), paragraph symbols (¶), registered trademark (®), section (§), and trademark (™). Within the MARKERS submenu are methods to indicate the current page number, the previous and next page numbers, as well as the current section number. HYPHENS & DASHES has shortcuts for creating an Em Dash (—) and En Dash (–) and discretionary hyphens for when a hyphen needs to placed somewhere other than where InDesign thinks one should go. QUOTATIONS MARKS will place in double quotation marks (""), single quotation marks (''), straight quotation marks ("), or a straight apostrophe (').

Different sizes of white space can be placed between words or characters using the TYPE menu > INSERT WHITE SPACE. These include Em space (width of an uppercase M of the current typeface) an En space (width of an uppercase N of the current typeface) and fractional units of these spaces.

Many typefaces include extended characters that are not represented on a typical keyboard. To access the extended characters of a particular typeface, use the TYPE menu > GLYPHS **[FIG 37.1]** (also accessible from the WINDOW menu > TYPE & TABLES > GLYPHS). This panel will display all the characters in the chosen typeface along with any recently used glyphs. Different types of glyphs can be viewed by using the **Show** drop-down menu.

FIGURE 37.1   The Glyph window

To create a content frame from type, use the TYPE menu > CREATE OUTLINES. Any type within a selected text frame will be converted to vector outlines and can be modified with the direct selection tool (white arrow). Images or text can be used to fill the content frame. **[FIG 37.2]**

FIGURE 37.2   Outlined text with placed graphic

CHAPTER 38

Character and Paragraph Styles

Use the Character and Paragraph styles if consistent styles for type or paragraphs are to be used throughout a layout. The Character Style panel **[FIG 38.1]** (found under the WINDOW menu > STYLES > CHARACTER) can be used two ways—by defining the style first and then applying it or by selecting text that has already been typeset and then using that as the basis for a style. To create a new style, open the character style panel and click the Create new style icon at the bottom. A new style will be created called Character Style; double click the style to access the style controls. In the **General** setting, the style name can be changed as well as basing the style on a pre-existing style and defining a keyboard shortcut to apply the style. In **Basic Character Formats,** all standard type controls can be changed including font name and style, size, leading, kerning, tracking and case (normal, all caps, small caps, etc.) position (normal, superscript, subscript, etc.), as well as underlines and strikethroughs. **Advanced Character Formats** include horizontal and vertical scale, baseline shift, and skew. Color and line weight can be defined in the **Character Color** setting. Options for **Underlining** and **Strikethroughs** can be set in the Character Style Options as well. Once the character style is defined, text can be selected and the style can be applied to it; if changes are made in the character style panel, the text with style applied to it will be updated.

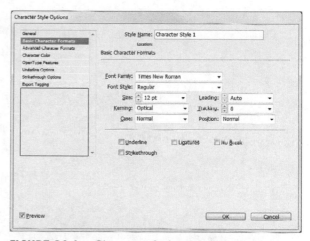

FIGURE 38.1   Character Styles window

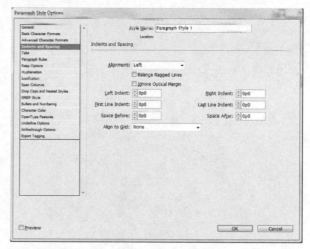

FIGURE 38.2   Paragraph Styles window

The second method involves selecting text that has been typeset (without a style applied) and then clicking the Create new style icon on the Character Panel. This will create a style based on the selected settings.

Paragraph styles work in a similar fashion but makes all of the adjustments to entire paragraphs as opposed to individual words or characters. The Paragraph Style panel **[FIG 38.2]** is found under the

WINDOW menu > STYLES > PARAGRAPH. Paragraph styles can change all the same characteristics as in the character style (leave the options in these blank as to not affect the character formatting) as well as all features related to paragraph formats. **Indents and Spacing**—essentially the entirety of the paragraph panel—includes controls for alignments, indents, space before and after, and alignment to the baseline grid. Options for tabs, hyphenation, and drop caps can also be found within the paragraph style options. Apply the styles the same way as the character styles—either select a paragraph and then apply the style or select a formatted paragraph to create a style from it.

CHAPTER 39

Text Wrap

Text wrap refers to the way text will wrap around an object, the control panel for this function is located under the WINDOW menu > TEXT WRAP. **[FIG 39.1]** The default option is **No Text Wrap [FIG 39.2]**—the object will not affect the type placed around it. The second option is to **Wrap Around the Bounding Box [FIG 39.3]**—in all instances in InDesign the bounding box is a rectangular frame no matter what the shape of the object. The controls include a distance from the edge of the content frame on the top, bottom, left, and right, which may be a positive or negative number. All the distances can be the same if the Chain link icon is selected or different if the icon is broken. Under wrap options, text can be wrapped to the **left, right,** or **both sides** of the content frame as well as **towards the spine, away from the spine,** or the **largest area** may be specified as well. The third option is to **Wrap**

Text Wrap
Invert
0p0
0p0
0p0
0p0
Wrap Options:
Wrap To: Both Right & Left Sides
Contour Options:
Type:
Include Inside Edges

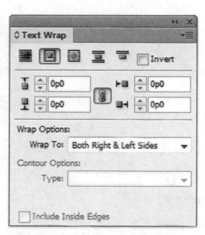

FIGURE 39.1 Text Wrap panel

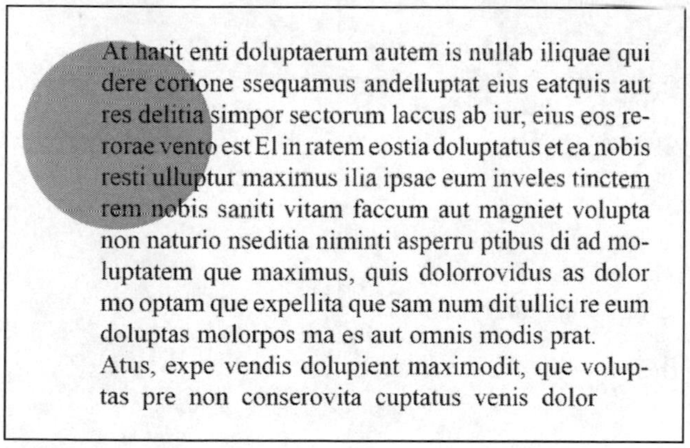

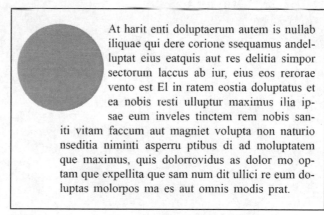

At harit enti doluptaerum autem is nullab iliquae qui dere corione ssequamus andelluptat eius eatquis aut res delitia simpor sectorum laccus ab iur, eius eos rerorae vento est El in ratem eostia doluptatus et ea nobis resti ulluptur maximus ilia ipsac eum inveles tinctem rem nobis saniti vitam faccum aut magniet volupta non naturio nseditia niminti asperru ptibus di ad moluptatem que maximus, quis dolorrovidus as dolor mo optam que expellita que sam num dit ullici re eum doluptas molorpos ma es aut omnis modis prat.
Atus, expe vendis dolupient maximodit, que voluptas pre non conserovita cuptatus venis dolor

FIGURE 39.2 No Text Wrap

At harit enti doluptaerum autem is nullab iliquae qui dere corione ssequamus andelluptat eius eatquis aut res delitia simpor sectorum laccus ab iur, eius eos rerorae vento est El in ratem eostia doluptatus et ea nobis resti ulluptur maximus ilia ipsae eum inveles tinctem rem nobis saniti vitam faccum aut magniet volupta non naturio nseditia niminti asperru ptibus di ad moluptatem que maximus, quis dolorrovidus as dolor mo optam que expellita que sam num dit ullici re eum doluptas molorpos ma es aut omnis modis prat.

FIGURE 39.3 Text wrapped around object bounding box

to the Object Shape. **[FIG 39.4]** If a rectangular shape is used, the controls will be the same as the bounding box wrap; for non-rectangular shapes there will be only one distance control. Under contour options, InDesign can use information derived from a placed graphic to determine the shape of the text wrap. The contour can be the same as the bounding box (the default) or can **detect the edges** of the graphic (e.g., for an image placed on a white background). A **predefined alpha channel** or **Photoshop Path** can be used as the contour as well. Use **Jump Object [FIG 39.5]** to have text end at the top of shape and continue below it. Use **Jump to Next Column** to have text end at the top of an object and continue in the next column or text frame. All contours created by text wrap can be manually edited using the direct selection tool (white arrow). The contour will appear as a lighter version of the current selection color.

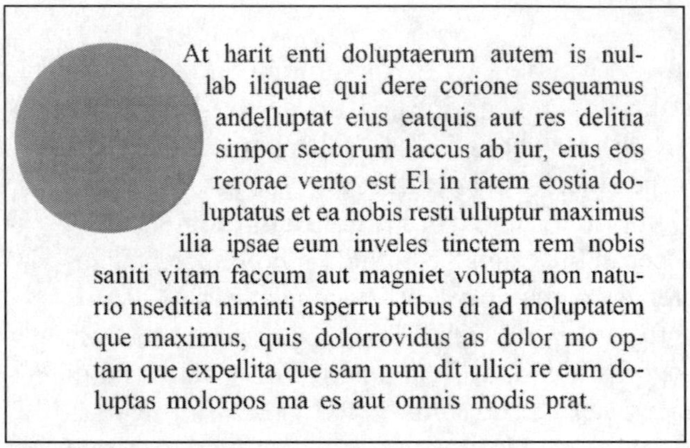

At harit enti doluptaerum autem is nullab iliquae qui dere corione ssequamus andelluptat eius eatquis aut res delitia simpor sectorum laccus ab iur, eius eos rerorae vento est El in ratem eostia doluptatus et ea nobis resti ulluptur maximus ilia ipsae eum inveles tinctem rem nobis saniti vitam faccum aut magniet volupta non naturio nseditia niminti asperru ptibus di ad moluptatem que maximus, quis dolorrovidus as dolor mo optam que expellita que sam num dit ullici re eum doluptas molorpos ma es aut omnis modis prat.

FIGURE 39.4   Text wrapped around object shape

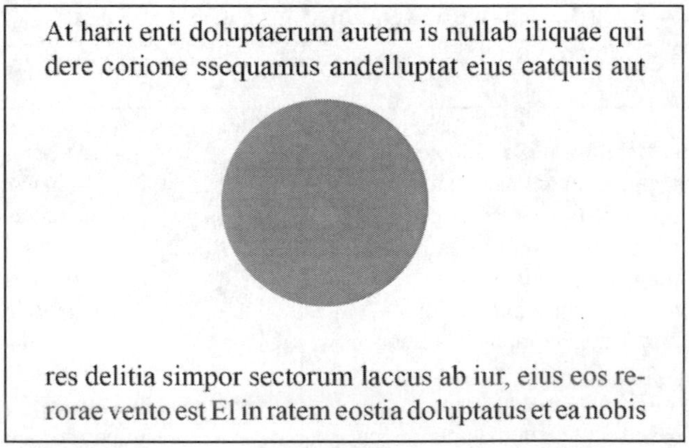

At harit enti doluptaerum autem is nullab iliquae qui dere corione ssequamus andelluptat eius eatquis aut

res delitia simpor sectorum laccus ab iur, eius eos rerorae vento est El in ratem eostia doluptatus et ea nobis

FIGURE 39.5   Text Jumping the object

CHAPTER 40

Effects

Full Effects controls can be found under the OBJECT menu > EFFECTS **[FIG 40.1]** or the WINDOW menu > EFFECTS. **[FIG 40.2]** Effects include transparency, drop shadows, inner shadows, outer glow, inner glow, bevel and emboss, satin, basic feather, directional feather, and gradient feather. These can be used individually or multiple effects can be selected. When an object is selected the effect can be applied to the object as a whole or its individual components including strokes, fills, graphics, and text. Each of these components may be treated separately by selecting the component in the **Setting for** dropdown in the OBJECT > EFFECTS window or by selecting the **component** in the WINDOW > EFFECTS panel. The **transparency** will make changes to the overall transparency of the object or individual components and can also affect the blending mode in a manner similar to Photoshop's blending modes. **[FIG 40.3]**

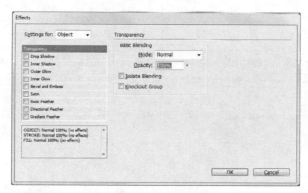

FIGURE 40.1 The Effects window

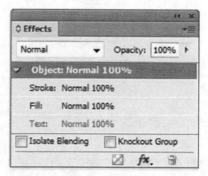

FIGURE 40.2 The Effects panel

FIGURE 40.3A Drop shadow applied two ways. On the left, a drop shadow with the size of the shadow set to 5; on the right a drop shadow with a size set to 0 and a smaller offset

FIGURE 40.3B Inner shadow—the effect can make text appear as if it makes a hole in the page

FIGURE 40.3C Outer glow—a soft glow emanating from the text. The size of the glow can be set to 0 to make a crisp edge.

FIGURE 40.3D Inner glow—a glow on the inside of the text

FIGURE 40.3E Bevel and emboss—creates a 3D effect

FIGURE 40.3F Satin—makes text appear covered in satin

FIGURE 40.3G Basic feather—blurs all edges the same

FIGURE 40.3H Directional feather—blurs all of the edges differently; includes settings for top, bottom, left, and right and angle of the effect and whether it is applied to the whole shape or individual edges

FIGURE 40.3I Gradient feather—uses a gradient to control the feathering; includes a gradient ramp and angle control